Population Ageing, Migration and Social Expenditure

Population Ageing, Migration and Social Expenditure

José Alvarado

Principal Research Officer, Multicultural Affairs Unit, Victorian Department of the Premier and Cabinet, Australia

and

John Creedy

The Truby Williams Professor of Economics, University of Melbourne, Australia

Edward Elgar
Cheltenham, UK • Northampton, MA, USA

Published by
Edward Elgar Publishing Limited
8 Lansdown Place
Cheltenham
Glos GL50 2HU
UK

Edward Elgar Publishing, Inc.
6 Market Street
Northampton
Massachusetts 01060
USA

A catalogue record for this book
is available from the British Library

Library of Congress Cataloguing in Publication Data

Alvarado, José, 1956–
      Population ageing, migration, and social expenditure / José
Alvarado, John Creedy.
      Includes bibliographical references.
      1. Aged—Government policy—Economic aspects. 2. Immigrants—
Government policy—Economic aspects. 3. Emigration and
immigration—Economic aspects. 4. Demographic transition—Economic
aspects. 5. Age distribution (Demography)—Economic aspects.
6. Expenditures, Public. 7. Social policy. 8. Australia—Social
policy. I. Creedy, John, 1949–   . II. Title.
HV1451.A58   1998
304.6'0994—dc21
                                                                                      97–37218
                                                                                      CIP

ISBN1 85898 724 5

Printed and bound in Great Britain by
Biddles Ltd, Guildford and King's Lynn

Contents

List of Figures

List of Tables

Acknowledgements

Part of the research reported here was supported by a grant from the former Bureau of Immigration, Multicultural and Population Research. Some early results appeared in Alvarado and Creedy (1996) *Migration, Population Ageing and Social Expenditure in Australia* (Canberra: AGPS). Research for chapter 11 was supported by an ARC Small Grant. Some of the material in chapters 2 and 7 is based on the introduction to Creedy (ed.) (1995) *The Economics of Ageing* (Aldershot: Edward Elgar). We have received helpful comments on drafts of various parts of this book, from Clive Brooks, Antonia Cornwell, Norman Gemmell, Rajat Sood and Mark Wooden. Substantial editorial and word-processing help in producing the camera-ready copy was provided by Kath Creedy.

Part I

Introduction

Chapter 1

Introduction and Outline

1.1 Ageing and Social Expenditure

The major industrialised countries are undergoing a significant demographic transition associated with low fertility rates combined with reduced mortality rates. This is the latest stage in a series of demographic transitions taking place over a long period of time, starting from a combination of high fertility and high mortality, through a period of high fertility combined with a substantial reduction in mortality rates. An implication of the current transition is that the population is expected to age substantially, although this effect is not anticipated until the second and third decades of the twenty-first century. There are obviously many causes and consequences of such population ageing, but it is not the purpose of this study to provide a comprehensive analysis of the wide range of factors involved or to attempt an overall evaluation.

This study focuses on the possible effects of population ageing on social expenditure, and examines the role of immigration in influencing both these factors. Social expenditure considered in this study consists of those items of expenditure which vary with age. These are age pensions, other age assistance, unemployment benefits, other social security benefits, health, education and employment. Total government social expenditure on people aged 75 and over is five times higher than public outlays on people under 16 years of age; in the case of health expenditure that ratio is 13 to 1. Major influences on social expenditure are the size and structure of the population, changes in social policy which cause outlays in various government spending programmes to change, and real increases or decreases in outlays due to factors other than policy changes. Population ageing means that some items of social expenditure fall while others are expected to rise; hence the precise extent to which aggregate expenditure may vary is far from clear.

The possible implications of population ageing for social expenditure have been recognised as an important subject of study for some time. This is not surprising given that the main features of the population age structure can be expected to change in reasonably predictable ways and are not subject to erratic changes. Furthermore, social expenditure now forms a very large proportion of total government expenditure, and is particularly difficult to control. Expenditure predictions have been made for a variety of countries by international organisations such as the International Monetary Fund (IMF) and the OECD; see Heller *et al.* (1986) and Hagemann and Nicoletti (1989). Studies of social expenditure in Australia have been made by Kelley (1988), Economic Planning Advisory Council (EPAC) (1988, 1994) and Creedy and Taylor (1993a, 1993b).

These studies typically find that the ratio of social expenditure to Gross Domestic Product (GDP) is projected to be lower in Australia than in many other countries. A major reason why Australia differs from the majority of OECD countries is the influence of high immigration levels. This has the effect of slowing down the extent of population ageing.

In considering social expenditure, the impact of immigration is not restricted to its demographic effects. Differences in social and economic characteristics between immigrants and the existing population may alter the propensity to use social services and hence the ratio of social expenditure to GDP. These social and economic characteristics are associated with the national origin of migrants, which has changed during recent decades. For instance, people born in the UK and Ireland contributed 53.3 per cent of the total number of migrants to Australia in 1964-65, whereas in 1994-95 they represented only 13.3 per cent of the total migrant intake. People born in the former Yugoslavia and Viet Nam contributed 13.4 per cent of the total number of migrants to Australia in 1994-95. The general trend in the inflow of migrants to Australia has been towards an increasing participation of people born in countries where English is not the main language. This trend is likely to continue.

In studying the effects of population ageing, with the associated role of immigration, on social expenditure in Australia, it is therefore advisable to consider both the demographic and the socio-economic characteristics of migrants. Given the increasing heterogeneity in the birthplace composition of the migrant intake and the association between birthplace and socio-economic characteristics, these factors represent a potentially important dimension of the analysis.

The aim of this study is to extend the previous analyses in two major ways. First, analyses typically use official population projections. Such projections are made for a limited range of assumptions concerning immigration levels. This study produces new projections for a much wider range of assumptions about immigration.

The second major difference relates to the treatment of immigrants in producing population projections and in measuring social expenditure. In particular, previous studies make the strong assumption that immigrants immediately acquire the demographic and economic characteristics of the rest of the population. In other words, it is assumed that they have the same mortality and fertility characteristics, as well as the same labour market characteristics, such as labour force participation and unemployment rates, as everyone else. In contrast, this study allows for a certain amount of population heterogeneity both in the production of population projections and those of social expenditure costs. Hence, the following analysis allows for variations in the composition of the population over time under alternative assumptions regarding immigration levels. The major distinction used is between immigrants from non-English-speaking backgrounds and immigrants from English-speaking backgrounds. This broad classification is frequently made in studies of the socioeconomic and demographic characteristics of immigrants.

1.1.1 Some Qualifications

In order to avoid any misunderstanding it is perhaps worth stressing that the analysis is strictly limited to being an exercise in demographic and economic measurement. For example, the results take the form of a descriptive statement that, under a specified set of assumptions, a given change in immigration is associated with a particular change in the age structure of the population and has consequent implications for social expenditure, measured in relation to GDP. This type of statement should not be interpreted in any way as a policy statement or value judgement. Immigration is associated with a wide range of causes and consequences, and many of these lie outside the special expertise of economists. The analysis simply represents an attempt to attach some orders of magnitude to a limited range of economic variables. These measures can provide a component of a wide-ranging policy debate. It is argued that, in view of the complexity and the large number of factors involved, these orders of magnitude are far from being immediately obvious. A serious and unbiased attempt at measurement is better than vague guesses and exaggerated claims that would otherwise be made in connection with a particular policy argument. Rational policy debate requires appropriate projections rather than guesswork. The projections have the substantial advantage that all the underlying assumptions are made explicit.

The ratio of social expenditure to GDP gives some idea of the amount of taxation that needs to be raised in order to finance the expenditure. Projections showing an increasing ratio of expenditure to GDP indicate that, in the absence of increased government borrowing or changes to eligibility conditions or levels of benefits, a corresponding increase in tax revenue is needed. This is because social expenditures are financed on a pay-as-you-go basis. There is, for example, no social insurance fund in Australia. However, higher tax rates may not necessarily be needed depending on the extent to which the tax system has built-in flexibility.

This study does not consider the revenue aspects, but a word of caution is required regarding the interpretation of expenditure ratios. Too often, commentators regard the ratio of expenditure to GDP as a measure of the burden imposed on the working population, although the precise meaning of the word 'burden' is seldom discussed. A full-scale study of the precise redistributive implications, between and within several generations, of all taxes and benefits is required before making any assertion about burdens.

A distinction must also be drawn between the types of projection reported here and economic forecasts that are made on the basis of a statistical or econometric model. Such models are concerned with forecasts of variables that are essentially arithmetic means, or 'expected values', of specified conditional distributions. Hence probability statements, or 'confidence limits', can be attached to any forecasts. The population and social expenditure projections reported in this study are not based on statistical relationships. They require extensive assumptions about fertility and mortality, as well as factors such as unemployment, labour force participation and productivity, and the way in which all these variables change over the projection period. The variables, particularly the economic ones, can change in substantial and unpredictable ways that cannot possibly be known over such a long period. Migration levels, as well as the composition of migrants, can change over time for a complex variety of reasons. Indeed, the government is unable to control the precise number of immigrants, and can only control the set of conditions under which individuals qualify for entry.

There are also interdependencies which are extremely difficult to allow for in making projections. For example, the inward and outward migration flows may be expected to depend to some extent on the growth of real incomes in Australia relative to other countries, and productivity in turn may depend on the number and composition of migrants. Similarly, the need to finance any expenditure level using various forms of taxation may itself produce effects on the labour market, and even fertility and migration, that are extremely difficult to model. The projections here are more appropriately described as arithmetic exercises; they give the population and social costs associated with particular assumptions regarding immigration. In this situation the best that can be done is to consider the sensitivity of the results to variations in some of the underlying assumptions. The claim of this study is simply that it extends previous exercises in the ways already indicated.

1.2   Outline of the Book

The following chapters are arranged in three Parts. Part II provides an introduction to some of the main issues concerning population ageing and migration. It provides a partial review of the literature on population ageing and immigration with the aim of providing some background and a general introduction to the later analyses. Part II is made up of three chapters. Chapter 2 discusses the demographic and economic aspects of the transition towards an older population which is being experienced by the major industrialised countries. Previous types of demographic transition are also discussed. Chapter 3 discusses the economic consequences of population ageing. It examines, in particular, the possible impacts of ageing on government budgets and the labour market. Chapter 4 turns to a discussion of some of the economic, social, and demographic issues related to immigration and the country of origin of migrants.

Part III takes a closer look at the structure of the Australian population and immigration. It can be said to provide the rationale for the particular approach undertaken in this study, that is, the allowance for a certain amount of population heterogeneity in the production of both population and social expenditure projections. To achieve this objective, chapter 5 compares the main demographic characteristics of the Australian population, where individuals are distinguished by their birthplace. Chapter 6 examines the influence of country of origin on several socio-economic indicators, particularly those which are most relevant in explaining government social expenditure.

Part IV presents the main substantive contribution of this book. It provides population and social expenditure projections under a variety of assumptions concerning the number and composition of immigrants. This Part begins in chapter 7 with a description of the models used to make the population and social expenditure projections. Chapter 8 presents two sets of population projections. The 'benchmark' population projections, for various immigration levels, are made under the standard assumption of population homogeneity. These are compared with additional projections made under the assumption of population heterogeneity. Chapter 9 briefly describes the components and nature of the social expenditure system in Australia. Chapter 10 presents the social expenditure projections. These mainly take the form of projections of the ratio of social expenditure to gross domestic product, which is obtained under the alternative assumptions of ignoring the composition of the population and under the population decomposition approach. The projection models of chapter 7 are 'deterministic' in that they simply produce the population structure and social expenditure ratios under alternative assumptions regarding a large range of variables. Chapter 11 provides an investigation of the statistical properties of these social expenditure projections with the use of a stochastic model.

The emphasis of the applied work in this book is on the Australian economy. This presents an interesting case study in view of the high levels of migration experienced, particularly over the last fifty years. However, the techniques developed in order to produce the projections, including the method of allowing for population heterogeneity and the introduction of stochastic elements into the model, can be applied without modification to any other country.

Part II

Population Ageing and Migration

Chapter 2

Demographic Transitions

Everyone is necessarily aware of individual ageing. The division of the life cycle into a number of distinct stages has been recognised for many centuries. While the individual ageing process has for long played a prominent role in some other disciplines, extensive investigations into the economics of ageing are relatively recent, and in many countries there are still relatively few published data containing decompositions according to age or life-cycle stages.

An important distinction must be drawn between individual and population ageing. The latter concerns the age distribution of the population. It is influenced more by fertility patterns than by mortality or longevity characteristics of individuals. It might be thought that, in view of the importance of the population model associated with the famous work of Malthus, concern with population ageing would stem at least from the early classical economists. However, the major area of interest was rapid population growth even though changes in death rates were recognised as important; concern for ageing is relatively modern. The analytics of population growth and age structure were not explored at length until the early years of the present century. Furthermore, in view of the early age at death of the large majority of people, population growth was regarded by the classical economists as being synonymous with labour force growth, so that no independent role was attached to the age distribution.

Population ageing represents just one stage which many industrialised countries are likely to experience in the early years of the next century, having previously passed through several previous stages or demographic transitions. The nature of these transitions has implications for the development of social insurance arrangements. The World Bank (1994) estimated that in 1990 almost 500 million people, that is, more than 9 per cent of the world's population, were aged 60 years and over, and by 2030 the number of people in this age group may reach 1.4 billion. Most of this growth in the number of older people will occur in developing countries.

This chapter discusses the main elements involved in the demographic transition towards an older population, and the relationships between demographic transitions and economic factors. Section 2.1 focuses on the demographic transition theory, whose main tenets are discussed and criticised. Section 2.2 discusses further the relationships between demographic transitions and economic growth. The main research findings on the relationships between economic growth, fertility and mortality are presented. Similarly, the effects of demographic transitions and economic growth on family structure and living arrangements are discussed.

2.1   The Demographic Transition Theory

Individuals age inexorably from birth to death. Population ageing, on the other hand, is not necessarily a continuous process. The ageing of a population can be reversed or at least retarded through changes in its age structure. The age of a population is measured by the proportion of people in different age groups or, alternatively, by the arithmetic mean or median age of the population. Changes in fertility, mortality and international migration can affect the age structure of a population and, therefore, its ageing process. This section examines the process through which these demographic variables interrelate and lead towards an older population age structure. The framework used to explain this process of population ageing is that of the demographic transition theory.

It is possible to distinguish several demographic stages or transitions through which most industrialised societies have been observed to pass.

Table 2.1: Demographic Transitions

	Pre-modern	Early	Later	Modern
Births/1000	45	45	45	20
Deaths/1000	40	33	15	10
% 15 years and under	36	38	45	26
% 60+ years	5	5	5	15
Expectation of life at birth	25	30	50	70
Population growth rate	0.5	1	3	1

Studying the European historical pattern of mortality and fertility rates, demographers developed the 'demographic transition theory'; a synthesis of the main tenets of this theory was presented by Notestein (1953). The theory of demographic transition explains the demographic changes experienced by societies as they evolve from a 'primitive' stage, which is characterised by a population equilibrium of high mortality and fertility, to a 'modern' stage of development during which a new equilibrium of low mortality and fertility is reached.

The time taken to move through the various stages has, however, varied between countries, and there is evidence to suggest that more recently industrialised countries have passed through some later stages relatively more quickly. The different stages are characterised mainly by their birth and death rates (expressed per 1000 of the population) and the associated age distribution of the population. Table 2.1 summarises the characteristics of the demographic transition under four main headings. The figures given in the table must be regarded simply as representative values rather than indicating precise orders of magnitude for a particular country.

The pre-modern stage is characterised in Table 2.1 by quite high fertility and high mortality. The expectation of life at birth is only about 25 years, so there are very few individuals in the 'over 60' age group. The high birth rate, while imposing very heavy burdens on families, is nevertheless associated with a growth rate of the total population of only about half of one per cent, so that reproduction is sometimes described as being very inefficient.

The middle two stages are shown as 'early transition' and 'later transition' periods, though they are sometimes amalgamated into a single demographic transition, or movement towards the 'modern' period. The early transition period is characterised by a fall in mortality, particularly infant mortality, which is associated with a rise in the expectation of life to about 30 years. In the later transition period, improved health conditions reduce mortality and increase longevity further, while the birth rate continues to be high. This period is thus associated with a high youth dependency ratio, with about 45 per cent of the population under the age of 15 years. Despite the much higher expectation of life at birth, the proportion of people over 60 years remains relatively low, while the population growth rate is increased to about 3 per cent. Indeed, it can be shown that the extent of population ageing is more sensitive to fertility than to mortality changes.

The later transitional period is one in which the idea of retirement from employment does not really exist, despite the increased longevity. Individuals continue to work, unless illness prevents labour market participation. For example, during this transitional period in Britain, the various Friendly Societies were able to cope with the requirements of such sickness insurance for their members, and were well placed to handle the potential moral hazard problems. Hence increased longevity did not lead to a breakdown of family support systems, despite the high youth dependency ratio already faced.

As shown in Table 2.1, the modern period experiences a continued reduction in mortality and an increase in the expectation of life at birth to about 70 years. A significant feature is the reduction in the birth rate so that, despite the extra longevity, the population growth rate falls to about 1 per cent. The age composition of the population shifts dramatically, with a reduction in the proportion below 15 years and an increase in the proportion aged over 60 years. For instance, between 1850 and 1950 life expectancy at birth in the US increased from 40 to 68 years; see Fogel (1994, p.383). Fries (1980) argued that mortality and morbidity were being compressed towards the limit of human life producing a 'rectangularisation' of the survival curve, as well as of the population age structure, with older people expected to live healthier lives until their biological limits are reached. Fries (1980) suggested a biological limit of 85, plus or minus 7 years; see Rowland (1991a, pp.43-

46). However, more recent medical advances have brought about further mortality declines particularly for people aged 65 and over. This questions the notion of a biologically fixed life span, suggesting that if it is fixed, the limit is well above 85 years. Fogel (1994, pp.383-384) outlines the controversy surrounding this issue.

These later transitions place great strain on family support systems, given the difficulty of making life-cycle savings, despite the reduction in the youth dependency ratio. In Britain, the significance of these changes was not at first fully appreciated by the Friendly Societies, who were initially opposed to the introduction of government Old Age Pensions. But the demand for some kind of government pension became irresistible in the major industrialised countries at the turn of the century. The shift from family support to government support in the form of the tax and transfer system involved a complex range of factors, including the very high costs, particularly health costs, of supporting the aged compared with those of supporting the young. Hence the overall burden of dependency increased despite the reduction in birth rates.

The modern period shown in Table 2.1 corresponds to the industrialised countries around 1960, and must be augmented by a yet more modern or post-modern period through which many countries are currently passing. The expectation of life at birth has increased further and it has been found that the support costs (again particularly health costs) rise dramatically for individuals over 75 years, who form a growing proportion of the population. The birth rates have also fallen further, implying significant population ageing in the early years of the twenty first century. This population ageing is also associated with the ageing of the members of the postwar baby boom. The implications of the more recent demographic transition are, however, more complicated than is often thought in popular debates.

The recent post-modern period has also seen a substantial increase in the labour force participation rate of women (partly associated with the lower birth rate) along with a certain amount of variability in unemployment rates. Following a shift of the 'aged burden' to the tax and transfer system during the modern period, the commonly expressed fear is that future working populations will renege on the implicit social contract between generations. Inter-generational equity issues are therefore now receiving some attention from economists. It is also of interest that, despite the much lower birth rate, more recent times have seen increased pressure from some quarters for a further shift of the 'youth burden' to the tax and transfer system. Others have expressed concern over such a shift, partly associated with what some commentators have referred to as a breakdown of the nuclear family. Many of the industrialised countries may be regarded as entering a territory whose characteristics are very difficult to predict. The demographic transition is nevertheless likely to involve a continued transition in social insurance arrangements which have experienced very little stability in their short history.

It has been mentioned earlier that an increase in longevity in the industrialised countries led to a demand for the introduction of some kind of government age pension and health insurance scheme. The difficulty of providing adequate personal savings for old age, combined with the strain placed both on family support and the existing sickness support schemes, which covered only a small minority of workers, resulted in a situation in which the aged formed the vast majority of those found to be living below a designated poverty level. At about the same time, there was much wider recognition of a role for the government in the other areas of social insurance, such as sickness and unemployment. It is no accident that this movement coincided with wider support for redistribution, involving also the use of progressive income taxation.

Social insurance schemes are typically financed on a pay-as-you-go (PAYG) basis, that is, from current taxation, and pensions form by far the largest component of social expenditure. A variety of market failure arguments have been advanced to justify the use of such social insurance. In addition, the inter-generational transfers involved in PAYG pension schemes are often described in terms of an implicit social contract between three generations: each generation stands to gain from such an arrangement so long as there is sufficient productivity and population growth. The increased ageing of the population, expected to be most prominent in the early years of the next century, has been widely anticipated as placing great strain on this metaphorical contract. Pensions and health are not, however, the only age-related forms of social expenditure, and the implications of population ageing for aggregate social expenditure are far from clear, given the many elements involved.

2.1.1 Limitations of the Transition Theory

The basic tenets of the demographic transition theory rest on the European experience. The predictive capacity of the theory as such is influenced by cultural and regional factors, as well as by the process of development itself, which assumes specific characteristics depending on the country and period considered. Some of the weaknesses of the demographic transition theory, in its original formulation, include the assumption that there is no population change before and after the transitional period, the almost exclusive concentration on fertility as a dependent variable, and the implicit treatment of each country as an independent unit.

In studying contemporary experiences of demographic transitions, Chesnais (1992) found that nothing precludes the appearance of significant population changes before and after the transitional period, with the populations of some countries experiencing different degrees of ageing and growth. Similarly, fertility and mortality do not seem to act independently, as suggested by the demographic transition theory. Chesnais (1992) argued that there is a long-term interdependence between mortality and fertility. Mortality decline eventually leads to a fertility decline, with the two changes working together in a complex interplay. The relative decline in infant and juvenile mortality may initially offset fertility declines while they are still small. He argued (1992, p.286) that:

> as soon as declining fertility gains momentum, and most of what can be accomplished in terms of combating juvenile mortality has been achieved, the base of the pyramid rapidly contracts. After all, birth control within families tends to be adopted when the number of children, owing to the progressive elimination of the chances of infant mortality, becomes too costly to support. Moreover, if such fertility declines occur in smaller generations,

the contraction at the foot of the pyramid is reinforced by an echo effect (as successive small generations reach reproductive age) and ageing is more rapid.

Considering each country as an independent unit, the demographic transition theory assumes that demographic changes are caused only by internal developments. This excludes the mechanisms through which demographic changes diffuse from country to country, such as the impact of international migration as well as the effect of improvements in communications and the worldwide spread of technological advances. According to the World Bank (1994), the faster spread of medical progress and rapid fertility declines are accelerating demographic transitions in developing countries. For example, in Belgium the proportion of the population over 60 doubled from 9 to 18 per cent over a period of more than 100 years, but it is estimated that the same transition in Venezuela will take only 22 years. Developing countries are expected to have 'old' demographic profiles at much lower levels of per capita income than the industrial nations. The impact of mortality declines on the demographic ageing of developing countries may increase in the near future as medical advances in developed countries tend to concentrate more on the elimination of illnesses of old age.

It may also be argued that migration provides a mechanism for relieving population pressures. Migration provides a means of escaping crisis and, in that sense, there may be a substitution of mortality by migration. Although international migration is absent from the theory of demographic transition, migratory movements played a role in the demographic transitions experienced by European countries. Indeed, migration is a major feature of nineteenth century European demography. Chesnais (1992, p.153) suggests that between 1815 and 1914 over 60 million Europeans, comprising over 20 per cent of the population in 1850, left their country of origin. The selectivity of the migration process may also have had important demographic implications, particularly because migrants quite probably had lower mortality rates than non-migrants. Furthermore, migration is often concentrated among young adults, who have high reproductive potential.

International migration may also involve a levelling of demographic and economic conditions between countries. Hence, it has formerly helped Europe solve its social problems and now relieves, though to a much lesser extent, the poverty of some countries. This ensures a greater aggregate population than otherwise; see, for example, Chesnais (1992, p.186).

A further strand in demographic theory, initially associated with the writings of Becker (1981) and Schultz (1988) is that of economic demography. This has been trying to develop a comprehensive account of the factors influencing fertility behaviour, particularly among the people living in the poorest regions of the world. The interaction between population growth and the environment has been recognised since Malthus, though he referred only to agricultural land. But economic demographers have been using household decision-making models, regarding population growth as endogenous. Such models are used to examine the relationship between population growth, environmental degradation and poverty.

In studying the situation of the Indian subcontinent and sub-Saharan Africa, Dasgupta (1993, 1995) presented an explanation of the population problem in those regions of the world. Modelling the household decision-making process in those regions, Dasgupta argued that large families are a survival strategy and that there exists a vicious circle which links poverty, environmental degradation and high fertility rates. He also cautioned that his findings could only have a bearing in the regions he studied, and suggested that a general theory of fertility behaviour is not currently available.

Other research on the population problem in developing countries is by Schultz (1994) who used data for 68 low-income countries over two decades to study the relationships between population growth, human capital and family planning. He concluded that schooling for women, rather than family planning, is the strongest factor in curbing population growth in those regions. Cropper and Griffiths (1994) studied the impact of population growth on deforestation in 64 developing countries in Latin America and Africa, and found that deforestation in those countries can be better explained as a problem of market failure, rather than one of population explosion. Timmer (1994) discussed policies to break the cycle of poverty and the population problem in developing countries.

2.2 Demographic Transitions and Economic Growth

Economic demography suggests that the demographic transition towards an ageing population is triggered by socio-economic developments, and is therefore a characteristic of the general development of societies. That is, demographic transition towards lower mortality and fertility rates, and the resulting ageing of the population, is a result of the social, economic, and technological development of societies. Higher income levels, educational attainments, biomedical achievements, a broadening of the social and economic opportunities for women and the promotion of welfare policies, have all combined to produce falling fertility and mortality rates.

2.2.1 Economic Growth, Fertility and Mortality

Studies based on cross-country data show strong correlations between fertility and economic growth; see, for example, Chesnais (1992) and Barro (1991). Several studies have tried to identify the mechanisms through which these variables are related. Becker and Barro (1988) argued that increased technological progress leads to a higher consumption growth rate and to a lower fertility rate; see also Galor and Weil (1996). Becker *et al.* (1990) found that in trying to provide children with high levels of human capital in societies with high levels of human capital and high rates of economic growth, it is optimal to have few children.

Other researchers have included gender issues in their models. Dasgupta (1995, p.1886) argued that gender inequality has an influence on fertility behaviour such that birth rates are expected to be lower in societies where women are more empowered. Education and, more importantly, opportunities for paid employment among women can empower them.

Galor and Weil (1996) used a model which links fertility decisions to relative wages for women and capital per worker. They established a positive feedback according to which increases in capital per worker lead to higher relative wages for women which, in turn, leads to lower fertility rates. Increases in savings, associated with higher wages, and lower population growth, lead to increases in the ratio of capital to labour. Their model can be used to explain demographic transitions and multiple equilibria. Thus, Galor and Weil (1996, p.376) argued that 'countries with a low initial level of capital per-worker may converge to a development trap where high fertility induces lower per-worker capital (through the "capital dilution" effect) and output, which in turn induces women, who confront low relative wages, to maintain their high fertility rate and low labor supply'.

The relationship between economic growth and lower mortality rates is also important in explaining population ageing, particularly because, as mentioned above, in modern societies mortality declines tend to concentrate in older age groups. High income is associated with a higher demand for and provision of health services and therefore with lower mortality rates. Moore *et al.* (1992) reported a long-run income elasticity of demand for medical services of around 1.5, based on econometric estimates across OECD countries; see Fogel (1994). The behaviour of mortality rates can have important implications on the provision and costs of services for the aged, particularly through their impact on the size of the elderly population. For example, Ahlburg and Vaupel (1990) estimated that if mortality at older ages continues to decline at 2 per cent a year, the US elderly population in 2050 could be 36 million larger than forecast by the Census Bureau.

2.2.2 The Impact on Family Structure

Demographic transitions and economic developments have also had an impact on the family structure and living arrangements of the population. In studying the amount of time devoted to the elderly by their children, Borsch-Supan *et al.* (1992) presented data on the changes in living arrangements among the elderly in the US during the post-war period. According to those figures, one in four elderly Americans lived alone in the 1940s, compared with more than 60 per cent in the late 1980s. Among those aged 85 and over, the proportion living alone increased from 13 to 57 per cent during the same period, while the rate of institutionalisation more than tripled.

High divorce rates, single households and childless couples are also more frequent in modern societies, particularly among the cohorts born during the post-war 'baby boom'. This has an impact on the family resources available to individuals as they age, particularly as a spouse is regarded as the most important family resource in old age. Similarly, female offspring are considered a valuable family resource for an aged parent, particularly for those living in financially precarious situations and unable to obtain paid help. It is estimated that 42 per cent of principal carers in Australia provide care to a partner and 28 per cent to a parent. Over half of the recipients are aged 60 years and over and 42 per cent of all male principal carers and 23 per cent of all female principal carers are also in this age group. Women, particularly between the ages of 35 to 64, are more likely than men to be providers of care. Of those providing care to a parent, 73 per cent are daughters and 27 per cent sons; see Australian Bureau of Statistics (ABS) (1996a, p.210).

The provision of care by women for an aged parent is concentrated among women aged 50 to 64. Caretaker ratios, which show the number of women aged 50 to 64 per octogenarian, have been calculated as a crude measure of the family resources available to the aged. Caretaker ratios have been declining in western countries and are expected to decline even more during the next few decades. In Australia, the caretaker ratio is expected to fall from 3.5 in 1986 to 1.8 potential carers per octogenarian in 2031; see Rowland (1991a, p.126). The potential availability of carers has also been affected by recent eonomic developments, particularly by the substantial increase in the labour force participation of women. In Australia, labour force participation rates of married women increased from 35.2 per cent in 1970 to 55.2 per cent at August 1995; see Norris and Wooden (1995, p.2).

The social and economic developments and the demographic transition towards an older population have weakened the traditional family support network of dealing with the aged. The reduction in family size, changes in living arrangements and the demands of modern society make it more difficult for the younger members of the family to care for the older ones. At the same time, 'ageing of the aged' produces a more fragile elderly population that requires specialised care.

Chapter 3

Economics and Population Ageing

The ageing process is accompanied by modifications in public expenditure and priorities for social policy. These changes have sometimes been depicted in exaggerated terms as acquiring the dimension of a worldwide crisis. For example, a pessimistic view was taken by the World Bank (1994, p.1) which stated in journalistic style that:

> Today, as the world's population ages, old age security systems are in trouble worldwide. Informal community- and family-based arrangements are weakening. And formal programs are beset by escalating costs that require high tax rates and deter private sector growth - while failing to protect the old. At the same time, many developing countries are on the verge of adopting the same programs that have spun out of control in middle- and high-income countries.

Some countries, particularly those of Europe, have already started to feel the economic strain associated with the ageing of their populations. For example, governments in those countries are spending an average of 9 per cent of their GDP on pensions. Projections for the richest economies show that public pension schemes will generate the greatest pressures on their government's budgets; see Leibfritz and Roseveare (1995).

The challenge to national economies posed by population ageing is two-fold, including the provision of adequate protection to the aged and the strain on society's resources derived from the ageing process. The provision of protection to the elderly, in terms of both income support and care, has traditionally been considered to be part of a social contract between several different generations. In that sense, one of the major issues of population ageing is its effect on public expenditures and the related issue of inter-generational fairness. But the economic effects of ageing are more widespread and interconnected. Population ageing has a significant impact on the labour market. Also, the ageing process may alter aggregate savings and consumption, investment, productivity, the external balances. There may, in addition, be some hidden costs. This chapter elaborates on those issues.

The analysis of the economic impact of ageing is divided into three sections. Section 3.1 focuses on the impact of ageing on government budgets, and begins with a brief discussion of the need for government intervention in the provision of care and support for the aged. Then three issues are discussed in more detail, namely the increase in fiscal deficits, the need for reform, and policies to address the budgetary impact of population ageing. Although the three life-cycle-related public expenditures are analysed, the discussion focuses particularly on the age pension, with education expenditure being given less attention. This is because the age pension seems to be the most serious issue for governments and the one upon which most research has been carried out.

Education expenditure is not expected to change much as a result of the ageing process, though investment in education can raise productivity, thereby helping to address the problems associated with the ageing of the population. Section 3.2 presents the labour market implications of population ageing, particularly the association of ageing with early retirement. Other economic implications of population ageing, such as its impact on savings and consumption, investment and productivity, external balances, and some hidden costs, are discussed briefly in section 3.3.

3.1   The Costs of Population Ageing

The demographic transition towards an older population, the reduction in
family size, increases in longevity, changes in living arrangements and demands of industrial societies, weaken the traditional family support network
of dealing with the aged. Although family-provided assistance continues to
play an important role, people tend to rely more on non-family resources to
face the contingencies associated with old age, particularly in terms of care
and income support. Government intervention is traditionally justified on
the grounds that the market fails to offer appropriate provision, and that
redistribution to the poor is usually needed. Creedy and Disney (1985) also
discussed paternalistic and fund-raising explanations of government intervention in the provision of social insurance.

Lindbeck (1995) argued that moral hazard and cheating are the weak-
est aspects of the welfare state, and that these weaknesses lead the welfare
state to face its basic dilemma, namely that the more generous the benefits,
the greater are the number of beneficiaries and the tax distortions created
to support the system. This leads to the emergence of vicious circles which
are strengthened by the impact of welfare state arrangements on short-term
macroeconomic dynamics. This involves the operation of automatic fiscal
stabilizers which, through unemployment benefits and other subsidies, lead
to larger budget deficits and government debts during recessions, higher interest rates, increased uncertainty and household saving rates, a still deeper
recession and so on. These vicious circles are further strengthened in the long
run when the corresponding habits and norms associated with welfare dependence have emerged. Lindbeck has referred to this in terms of 'hazardous
welfare state dynamics'.

Lindbeck (1995) argued that there seems to exist something of a 'welfare
state paradox'. That is, the welfare state arrangements which, unlike private
insurance schemes, are intended to protect the individual from the consequences of non-insurable situations, can be severely undermined where these
situations affect large parts of the population for prolonged periods, whether
these circumstances arise from macroeconomic shocks or from demographic

transitions towards older populations.

3.1.1   The Rise in Fiscal Deficits

The past few decades have witnessed the rise in fiscal deficits and public debts in developed countries. Although revenue collections in industrial countries taken together increased from an average of 28 per cent of GDP in 1960 to 44 per cent in 1994, expenditures increased even more dramatically, from 28 per cent to 50 per cent of GDP during the same period. The biggest increase occurred in transfers and subsidies, which from an average of around 8 per cent of GDP in 1960, increased to 21 per cent in 1992. As a result, the average gross public debt in these countries rose from 40 per cent to 70 per cent of GDP between 1980 and 1995; see IMF (1996, pp.44-46). Furthermore, this rise in fiscal deficits and public debt has occurred during a period characterised by demographic developments regarded as favourable for budget positions, namely, the postwar baby boom's entry into the labour force with relatively few retirees to support. This favourable demographic situation is rapidly changing, with population ageing making budgets prospects even worse.

Reflecting upon current concerns among economists regarding the impact of population ageing on government budgets, Haveman (1996) argued that there will be adverse effects on public sector deficits in the medium term in developed countries because of the resistance to increased taxation. However, over time there will be a fundamental reallocation of resources away from publicly funded support and towards private provision of health and retirement income support, eroding the social contract between generations. The increased fiscal pressures of population ageing will, it is argued, erode the availability of saving and investment, adversely affecting future economic growth.

The impact of population ageing on government budgets is two-fold. Population ageing is expected to increase some public expenditures, particularly expenditures linked to life-cycle developments, namely, age pensions and health. Education is a third item of demographically-linked government expenditure, but it is expected to change very little. At the same time, reductions in the proportion of working-age people will have a negative effect on fiscal revenues, making the extra expenditure harder to finance. The IMF (1996, p.53), assuming that current key pension parameters remain unchanged during the next few decades, estimated that, in net present value terms, government pension liabilities in 1994 exceeded 68 per cent of GDP in all major industrial countries, except the UK and the US. OECD (1995a, pp.35-36) projections of pension payments until 2070 show marked differences between the major industrial countries resulting from differences in the generosity of pension schemes and the elderly dependency ratios, with Japan, Germany, France and Italy the hardest hit by pension payments peaking at between 15 and 20 per cent of GDP with the ageing of the baby boom generation. Health expenditures are also projected to rise substantially, particularly in the US and Canada whose populations are ageing as well as growing.

3.1.2 The Need for Reform

The problems associated with persistent budget deficits are seen not only in terms of their impact on economic growth and the question of public debt sustainability in the long run, but also in terms of generational fairness. Hence, economists have been trying to develop methods of allowing a more appropriate measurement of the burden of fiscal policies on different generations while at the same time providing a better description of the policy changes needed to correct the distribution of such burdens. Auerbach *et al.* (1994 p.86) argued that 'generational accounting' is one such method. According to their calculations for the US, people born in 1900

> bore, on average, a lifetime net tax rate of about 22 per cent ... Under baseline policy, today's newborn generations will bear lifetime net tax rates of just under 34 per cent. But, as we already have learned, baseline policy is clearly unsustainable, leaving an enormous fiscal burden to be paid by future generations - equal to 71 per cent of their projected lifetime labor income!

Accordingly, welfare payments need to be overhauled to make them more sustainable and fair across generations.

Generational accounting exercises commissioned by the OECD for several industrial countries reached similar conclusions, but with significant differences in generational imbalances between countries according to differences in each country's extent of the ageing process and welfare policies as well as differences in the extent of the initial fiscal imbalance. Thus, assuming a discount rate of 5 per cent and productivity growth of 1.5 per cent, Italy's future generations are expected to have to pay net taxes more than five times as large as the current generation. In the US, future generations are expected to have to pay 100 per cent more net tax over their lifetimes. In Germany the extra burden is expected to be 25 per cent. Calculations based on alternative assumptions regarding productivity growth and discount rates also show a significant imbalance against future generations; see OECD (1995a, p.38).

Another issue related to intergenerational imbalance is that of cohort size. Some researchers argue that the size of the baby boom group has had a negative impact on earnings during the working lives of its members. Welch (1995), examining US wage and earnings data for the period 1967 to 1975, found evidence that large cohorts depress earnings and that most of the effect comes early in the career and increases with the level of schooling. Hence entry-level wages of college graduates from smaller cohorts can be expected to be higher than those of experienced workers and workers with less schooling; see Welch (1995, p.258). Similarly, Ferguson (1995) estimated the impact of changes of the age structure of the Canadian labour force on the income of different birth cohorts. He concluded (1995, p.285) that 'the baby boom group is likely to find its relative size working to its disadvantage through the bulk of its working life. The post-baby boom groups appear to do better, suggesting that their capacity to support a large retired population may be somewhat greater than recent discussions have implied'.

Cutler *et al.* (1995) go further in arguing that the baby boom generation in the US is less well off than the following generation because of the large cohort size. During their working years, wage growth is slow because of low capital to labour ratios, but during their retirement years, the rate of return on saving will be lower. Cutler *et al.* (1995, pp.222-223) also argue that, given productivity growth, the next generation will be more affluent than the current one, reducing the case for intergenerational redistribution from baby boomers in favour of their successors.

Currently, most public pension payments are financed on a pay-as-you-go (PAYG) basis; that is, current payments are funded by current contributions. A PAYG scheme is generally viewed as involving an implicit contract between three generations. Thus the working population agrees to pay the pensions of the retired population, on the understanding that their pensions will subsequently be paid by the next working generation. While this may sound comforting, it is of course entirely fictitious, and there is no general assurance that a scheme which is operated by one generation will be acceptable to subsequent generations; see Creedy and Disney (1985, p.51). The 'social insurance paradox', according to which social insurance can increase the welfare of each person if the sum of the rates of growth of population and real wages exceeds the rate of interest (see Aaron, 1966, p.372) is perhaps too simple a model to be applicable to any actual PAYG system.

Problems with PAYG schemes arise particularly when the population ages and schemes mature. Then, they produce economic inefficiencies and unintended intergenerational and intra-generational redistributions. The World Bank (1994) argues that a PAYG system produces low costs and large transfers to the first covered generations. It also produces transfers from later cohorts because of population ageing. It is argued that the largest transfers go to high-income groups in earlier cohorts, and a pay-as-you-go system also misses an opportunity for capital market development. For further discussion and examples of intergenerational and intra-generational redistribution in a PAYG system see Creedy and Disney (1985, pp.71-73).

Several commentators have argued that there is a welfare loss associatied with a PAYG system. Current benefits are paid out of current contributions; that is, the money collected is not invested, thereby missing the opportunity for capital market development and for obtaining a higher return on these contributions. Given that in a public PAYG system contributions are collected as, or adopt the form of, taxes, the deadweight loss of taxation

increases from the extra distortions. In the US, Feldstein (1996, p.13) found
that the payroll tax required by the current unfunded system distorts the
supply of labor and the form of compensation, raising the deadweight loss
of personal taxes. He also argued that each generation loses the difference
between the return to real capital that would be obtained in a funded system
and the lower return in the unfunded program.

It is often concluded that the current system is unsustainable. Measuring
the unsustainability of current public pension plans through the 'contribution
gap', that is, 'the difference between a constant sustainable contribution rate
that over a long period of time would lead to no build up of pension debt
above an initial level and the expected average contribution rate likely to
prevail under current law', the IMF (1996, p.54) concluded that all industrial
countries face contribution gaps over the period 1995 to 2050, with the typical
major industrial country projected to have an annual gap of 1.8 per cent of
GDP if nothing is changed.

Health expenditure is also increasing in most countries and will continue
to do so as the population ages, unless medical advances reduce illness in
old age. As people live longer, an increasing proportion survive to the age
when care is needed more and for longer periods, intensifying the strain on
the public purse.

3.1.3   Economic Policies

The OECD (1995a) has argued that the budgetary impact of population
ageing should be addressed through policies in three areas. These involve
the improvement of fiscal positions in the medium term through achieving
primary surpluses, the review of pension and health-care systems, and policies aimed at increasing the size of the workforce. Improving fiscal positions
before population pressures start to mount is regarded as one of the most
effective measures to deal with the budgetary impact of population ageing.
For example, Leibfritz and Roseveare (1995, p.36) estimated that a permanent cut in spending programmes of one percentage point of GDP in 2000
would result in net debt in 2030 being between 40-55 per cent of GDP lower

than otherwise in all of the countries considered, that is, the G7 countries.

Increases in labour force participation rates, in the retirement age and immigration can boost the workforce. Labour force participation of women has been increasing during the last two decades, particularly in countries where the employment share of the service sector is relatively large. However, falls in participation rates continues to be a common phenomenon for men, especially among the low-skilled; see OECD (1994, pp.28-33). There are practical limits to the use of immigration as an effective measure to offset falls in the size of the workforce.

Increasing working lifetimes has a two-fold advantage in alleviating budget pressures, namely, through increasing contributions paid and by decreasing the number of beneficiaries; however, there appears to be some labour market hostility towards older workers. *The Economist* (1996) reported that in an opinion poll taken throughout the European Union, 80 per cent of respondents of all ages believed that older workers, which can mean as young as 40, were discriminated against in job recruitment. Thus, raising the retirement age does not necessarily mean effective increases in the workforce.

Significant efforts to address the budgetary impact of population ageing need to be directed towards overhauling the pension and health care systems. Better design of health care systems and policies to achieve greater micro-efficiency are the two areas highlighted by the OECD as the most promising in terms of containing the growth of health expenditure resulting from population ageing; see OECD (1995a, p.40). Feldstein (1996, p.31) argued that 'the most fundamental challenge to any health-care system is to make the pattern of care responsive to individual preferences without imposing excessive financial burdens on individuals or denying necessary care because of inability to pay'. However, in studying alternatives to address the rapid growth of health expenditures it is also important to recognise that ageing is only one of the factors, and perhaps not the most important one, influencing health expenditure growth. For example, it is estimated that ageing population structures may have added only 0.2 per cent to the annual growth in health expenditure in the OECD area during the 1980s and 0.3 per cent during the early 1990s, compared with an OECD average real health expenditure growth of 3 per cent between 1980 and 1992; see OECD (1995b, p.95).

In considering alternative policy options to finance government pensions it is important to take several factors into account; see Creedy and Disney (1992) . One such factor is the aim of the pension system in regard to the income support it attempts to provide, that is the replacement ratio. A second factor is the interaction between the different components of the tax system and between them and the pension system. A third factor is the relationship between demographic dependency and economic dependency, with the latter including factors such as changes in labour force participation rates, in considering the impact of dependency ratios. In designing appropriate policy responses to rising pension costs it is also important to consider the implications arising from interrelationships between the dynamic factors involved. For example, a higher rate of population growth may lead to lower rate of labour force participation particularly among women of child bearing age, or a higher rate of growth of real wages may lead to higher participation rates. Reductions in population growth may lead to increases in productivity growth and labor force participation growth.

To face the pension problem, the IMF (1996) recommended increases in contribution rates and, particularly, expenditure reductions. With the latter taking the form of declines in replacement ratios and increases in the retirement age.

The World Bank (1994) argued that an old age security system should provide for three functions, namely saving, redistribution and insurance. It argued that the failure of traditional pension systems in providing security for the old as well as their inefficiencies and unsustainability are basically due to the fact that most pension systems combine the three functions in one dominant PAYG public pillar system. Thus, to overhaul the pension systems, the World Bank (1994, pp.15-16) recommended separating the saving and insurance from the redistributive functions and placing them under different financing and managerial arrangements in two mandatory pillars. One would be publicly managed and tax-financed, while the other would be privately managed and fully funded. These pillars would be supplemented by a voluntary pillar for those who want more. The public pillar would have the limited object of alleviating old age poverty and coinsuring against a multitude of risks.

The limited objective for the public pillar reduces the required tax rate. The second mandatory pillar, fully funded and privately managed, would link benefits actuarially to costs. It is argued that full funding should boost capital accumulation and financial market development, thereby increasing economic growth and making it easier to finance the public pillar. Voluntary occupational or personal saving plans would be the third pillar, providing additional protection for people who want more income and insurance in their old age. The World Bank believes that such diversification is the best way to insure against uncertainty.

3.2 Population Ageing and the Labour Force

The ageing and slowing of population growth produces an older and smaller labour force. The OECD estimated that during the next few years, population ageing will largely offset the positive impact on the size of the workforce resulting from increasing female labour force participation rates. Furthermore, although labour force growth is still projected to exceed population growth in most countries, a reduction in the labour force growth rate is expected between 1995 and 2005. The ageing of the labour force will increase, with over one worker in three expected to be older than 45 by 2005; see OECD (1994, p.26).

3.2.1 Population Ageing and Early Retirement

An associated problem is the trend towards declining labour force participation rates among older workers, that is people aged 55-64, particularly among men. In Australia, the labour force participation rate of full-time male workers aged 60-64 fell 32 percentage points between 1973 and 1993. This fall was concentrated in the first decade of the period; see Table 3.1, taken from ABS (1994b, p.126). Similarly, labour force participation rates among full-time male workers aged 55-59 dropped 22 percentage points during the last two

Table 3.1: Male Labour Force Participation Rates

Years	Age groups	Full-time	Part-time	Not in Lab force
1973	25-54	95.1	1.3	3.3
	55-59	85.9	2.4	11.7
	60-64	71.6	4.4	23.9
1983	25-54	90.8	3.2	6.0
	55-59	73.8	4.4	21.7
	60-64	38.2	4.6	57.2
1993	25-54	86.9	5.0	8.0
	55-59	63.8	6.5	29.8
	60-64	39.3	7.3	53.4

decades. Figures for 1992 collected by the ABS (1994b, p.127) show that 42.4 per cent of retired men aged 55 years and over had retired early, with almost one-quarter retiring between the ages of 55 and 59 years.

Both voluntary and involuntary reasons contribute to a person's decision to retire early. Among the latter, ill health or injury and labour market conditions are the main influences. Half of the retired Australian men aged 45 years and over gave ill health or injury as the reason for early retirement. In fact, men receiving a disability pension as a proportion of those not in the full-time labour force increased from 21 per cent to 40 per cent during the last decade for men aged 60-64 years, and from 34.2 per cent in 1983 to 41.0 per cent in 1987 for men aged 55-59 years; see ABS (1994b, p.128).

Trends toward higher rates and longer periods of unemployment discourage the participation of older men in the labour market. Between 1983 and 1993, the unemployment rate of men aged 60 to 64 increased from 7 per cent to 16 per cent. In 1993 the unemployment rate of men aged 55-64 years was 5 percentage points higher than that of younger men. Furthermore, in addition to experiencing longer unemployment durations, the likelihood of older men becoming long-term unemployed was almost four times higher than unemployed males between 25 and 54 years of age. It is not surprising that between 1983 and 1992 the proportion of retired men aged 45 years and over stating employment and other related factors as reasons for early retirement increased from 7.3 to 16.0 per cent (ABS 1994b, pp.127-129). Using survey data Borland (1995) argued that the decline in job opportunities rather than life-cycle choices was the primary reason for the fall in male, particularly older male, labour force participation rates during the 1980s; for further discussion see Kenyon and Wooden (1996) and Atkinson and Creedy (1997). The incidence of the labour market conditions on the decision to retire is usually complemented by early retirement incentives offered by the government and the private sector.

Voluntary early retirement is fundamentally related to the availability and attractiveness of sources of income other than labour. The ABS (1994b, p.127) found that in 1992, among men who had retired aged 55-64 years, 46 per cent had retirement schemes, investments or savings as their main source of income, and 42 per cent had government pensions and benefits. But of men who had retired aged 65 years or over, 28 per cent had retirement schemes, investments or savings as their main source of income, and 64 per cent had government pensions and benefits. In Australia it is apparently common practice for many of these retirees with superannuation cover to retire at 55 years of age with a lump sum which is used as an early retirement bridge, until they become eligible for a government pension. In fact, 50 per cent of persons retired between 1988 and 1992, most of them males, received a lump sum; while the proportion of retired men declaring a non-government main source of income in 1992 had fallen to 27.9 per cent from 38.5 per cent at retirement, and the proportion of those receiving government benefits had increased from 49.9 per cent at the moment of retirement to 64.1 per cent in 1992 (ABS 1994b, pp.144-145).

The extent of early retirement among men is expected to increase in the future for two main reasons. First, the increased superannuation coverage will give older workers, particularly high earners, more flexibility about their retirement decisions. However, measures to tighten eligibility criteria for the aged pension and legislation to prevent compulsory retirement on the basis of age may offset this effect to a certain extent; see EPAC (1996, p.46). Secondly, the fastest growth of the labour force is projected to occur for the 55 to 64 age group, whose share may increase from 7.4 per cent of the total labour force in 1993 to 11 per cent in 2011. Males aged 55 to 59 years are projected to experience the biggest fall in participation rates, of about 6 percentage points between 1993 and 2011; see ABS (1994g, pp.vi-vii). Nevertheless, declining male participation in the labour force may be offset somewhat by increasing female labour force participation, which is expected to continue to increase for all age groups.

Population ageing also brings about the problem of the level of qualification of the labour force. As the proportion of young people entering the labour force decreases, their contribution to increasing the skills of the workforce may fall, with the implication that more resources may have to be allocated to retrain older workers. For example, it is projected that by 2005 one quarter of Australians with higher education qualifications will be aged 45 to 59, an increase of 20 per cent from 1994, many of them having obtained their qualifications at younger ages. This raises the question of the relevance of the skills represented by those qualifications and the need for retraining and commitment to a process of lifelong learning; see Department of Employment, Education and Training (DEET) (1995, pp.73-74).

3.3   Other Economic Effects

Population ageing affects other economic variables; this section discusses briefly the most important of them, namely, savings and consumption, investment and productivity, the external balances, and some of what are called 'hidden' costs.

3.3.1   Savings and Consumption

The life-cycle hypothesis is the most popular framework to explain savings behaviour. According to this theory, borrowing and lending are undertaken to compensate for the lack of coordination between the timing of income and expenditures throughout the lifetimes of individuals. Thus, to pay for education and housing, individuals incur debt at young ages. During middle-age these loans are paid off and savings are created. These savings are then used in retirement.

Thus, if households behave as predicted by this theory, aggregate savings would be expected to fall as a result of population ageing. Although some studies, see for example Daniger *et al.* (1982), have shown that retirees do not dissave as the life-cycle theory postulates, especially during the first years of retirement, the evidence tends to support the theory. Weil (1989) has argued that aggregate savings may be reinforced by a bequest motive. Hurd (1992) used data from the Retirement History Survey (RHS) in the US and found no systematic difference between the consumption paths of parents and non-parents to support a bequest motive for saving. However, he concluded that the RHS data are consistent with the life-cycle hypothesis, with both consumption and saving falling after retirement. Nevertheless, falling saving rates as a result of population ageing is not expected to occur within the next few years, particularly in countries which still have relatively young populations. For example, Cutler *et al.* (1995, p.214) found that, because of the maturing of the baby boom generation, there will be a small increase in saving rates in the US during the next few decades.

The possible impact of population ageing on savings through social security pensions has also been analysed. Feldstein (1974) argued that through the 'asset substitution effect' social security pensions tend to reduce savings, but the longer retirement derived from the 'induced retirement effect' encourages savings during the shorter working period. Therefore, the net effect can only be determined at the empirical level.

3.3.2 Investment and Productivity

The reduction in labour force and relative increases in the ratio of capital to labour, due to the ageing and slowing of population growth in Western countries, have led some economists to predict reductions in investment and total output but increases in labour productivity; see, for example, Neal (1978). There have also been pessimistic arguments according to which the rate of technical progress is expected to fall as a result of ageing and the slowing of population growth; see Simon (1981) and Wattenberg (1987).

Taking an optimistic perspective, Cutler *et al.* (1995, pp.171-172) argued that slow labour force growth may induce more rapid technical change, suggesting that diminished fertility represents an opportunity rather than a problem. They found some evidence for this relationship, using data for 1960-1985. Their estimates suggest that the reduction in labour force growth projected for the next 40 years may raise productivity growth enough to offset increased dependence. However, they acknowledged that their finding is uncertain. A more definitive finding is the absence of any empirical support for the pessimistic view that ageing societies suffer reduced productivity growth.

3.3.3   Open Economy Effects

The demographic transition experienced by industrial countries is also expected to affect their relative external positions. Masson and Tryon (1995) studied the macroeconomic effects of population ageing in industrial countries and explained the open economy effects of ageing using the following argument. In a multicountry context, the ageing of the population of a country relative to the population of the other countries is important. Thus, for example, if the population of country A is relatively younger than that of country B, and if dependency ratios fall during the next ten years or so because the baby boom generation is still at working age while fertility rates are falling, then the saving rate in country A may increase (because of life-cycle saving behaviour of individuals) which is mirrored by a reduction in domestic demand. This will in turn reduce imports and lead to a real depreciation of its currency. On the other hand, the saving rate in country B will be falling, mirrored by increases in domestic demand, while at the same time country B's output is falling due to slowing labour force growth; this in turn will increase imports of country B, which means exports for country A. Thus, the current account of country A will improve, while at the same time the reduction in country A's domestic demand will be offset by an increase in demand for its exports due both to lower saving rates abroad and to a real depreciation of country A's currency. Therefore, the net foreign asset position of country A improves steadily and that of country B worsens.

These effects were used by Masson and Tryon (1995, p.586) to explain the future external balances of the US compared with other industrialised countries with older population structures. Their simulations showed that demographic shifts can be expected to have substantial effects on the global pattern of external balances over the next 35 years. In the US the net foreign asset position improves by over 35 per cent of GNP in 2025, compared, for example, with an assumed net debtor position in 1995 of about 23 per cent of GNP. In contrast, in Japan and Germany the net foreign asset positions in 2025 are lower than in 1995. They concluded that population ageing in the industrial countries has the potential to generate large swings in foreign indebtedness over time.

3.3.4 Hidden Costs

The loss of output and productivity associated with caring for elderly relatives, although very real, is difficult to measure and it is usually not taken into account when considering the economic impact of population ageing. A US study of employed people who also provided care for elderly relatives, cited by Barresi and Stull (1993, p.10), found that more than one-third of them experienced a worsening in work status after becoming a carer. As women are more often the carers, this represents an additional disadvantage for female participation in the labour force. A further possibility is that increased female labour force participation may decrease the number of informal carers and thereby increase the cost of formal care.

In Australia the ABS estimated that 83 per cent of people with severe or profound handicap, including 58 per cent of those aged over 80, live in households, with 60 per cent of them receiving informal assistance from a relative or friend. Of the 1.5 million family members and friends providing care, more than one-third were principal carers; see ABS (1993a and 1995). It is also estimated that in 1992 the value of this informal care was $3.4 billion; see Australian Institute of Health and Welfare (1995 and 1996).

Chapter 4

Immigration Issues

International migration plays a demographic and an economic role in most industrial countries. As with population ageing, the last decade has seen a considerable increase in research and public discussion on the economic implications of immigration, particularly in high immigration countries.

This chapter focuses on the main issues raised by international migration in the destination country. Section 4.1 discusses the economic consequences of immigration. First, the theoretical framework most commonly used in explaining the economic effects of immigration in the host country is presented. Then, the main research findings on the economic consequences of immigration are discussed. Although the discussion covers most economic issues, the emphasis is on the labour market implications of immigration. Section 4.2 presents other immigration issues, particularly those associated with the demographic role of immigration and the importance of the national origin of immigrants in explaining the success or failure of the migration experience.

4.1 Economic Consequences of Immigration

One model of the economic consequences of immigration is the neoclassical framework presented by Berry and Soligo (1969). The distributional effect of immigration can be explained using this model, although it is more often used to explain the impact of immigration on the national income of the host country. The model shows that if natives own the economy's fixed factors,

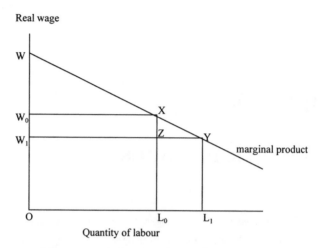

Figure 4.1: A Simple Model of Immigration.

then immigration increases natives' factor incomes through increasing returns to the owners of the fixed factors. Figure 4.1 illustrates this result.

The simple model illustrated in Figure 4.1 assumes that factors of production are paid their marginal products and natives own the economy's fixed factors, that is, land and capital. It is also assumed that immigrants do not bring capital with them, neither do they save and accumulate capital in the host economy after migrating. There is no government.

Figure 4.1 shows the economy's demand for labour, the variable factor, which is given by labour's marginal product. Before immigration occurs, and assuming the fixed factor is entirely owned by natives, the real income accruing to the owners of the fixed factor is represented by the area W_0XW. The total quantity of labour employed is OL_0 and its total real income is given by the area OW_0XL_0.

Assuming that immigrants only add to the supply of the variable factor and leave the quantity of the fixed factor as well as its ownership unchanged, the new employment level after migration is OL_1 and the economy's total income is now represented by the area OL_1YW, with the return per unit of the variable factor reduced to OW_1. Of the total income accruing to the variable factor, native workers receive OW_1ZL_0, which is lower than the income received by native workers before migration. Part of the native workers' pre-migration income, represented by the area W_1W_0XZ, is now accruing to the owners of the fixed factor, which has been made relatively scarcer by immigration. Immigrants, who are paid their marginal product, receive an income represented by the area L_0ZYL_1.

It is clear from Figure 4.1 that immigrants' contribution to output is greater than the payment they receive. This residual output is given by the area of the triangle XYZ and represents the net gain brought about by immigrants to the natives of the host economy. How this gain accrues to the various groups in the host country is a distributional issue which should be assessed separately from the overall gain from migration to the host society. In the two-factor model in the absence of redistributive mechanisms, the net gain from immigration accrues to the owners of the fixed factor.

According to this model, the economic benefits of immigration to the host country increases with the slope of the labour's marginal product curve, that is, with increases in the share of the fixed factor in aggregate output. The net economic gain from immigration decreases with foreign ownership of the fixed factor and with increases in the immigrants' share in the returns to both 'productive' capital used by immigrants on the job and the 'demographic' capital involved in the provision of services such as schools, hospitals and other welfare services.

It is important to stress that these results hold as long as the international movements of labour are independent of the international movements of capital. Moreover, as mentioned above, the model assumes that only labour moves between countries. Thus, immigration exerts a capital dilution effect in the host country. However, there is evidence to suggest that the international movements of capital are not independent of the international movements of labour. Furthermore, some studies argue that 'capital chases labour' internationally; see, for example, Clarke and Martin (1995).

Researchers have built upon the neoclassical framework to assess the economic consequences of immigration in the host country, though mixed results have been achieved. For example, Usher (1977) used a number of assumptions regarding the returns to capital obtained by immigrants to the UK and concluded that immigrants are a burden on UK natives. Following Usher, Peter and Verikios (1994) found that the 1991-92 intake of immigrants to Australia reduced the natives' incomes. On the other hand, Simon (1989) used an approach which separates the analysis of the 'production' capital used by immigrants in the job from the 'demographic' capital. He found positive economic effects of immigration in the US. Clarke and Ng (1991) and Tu (1991) have also concluded that immigration brings about economic benefits to the host country.

Within a neoclassical perspective, macroeconomic models have also been used to study the overall economic impact of immigration. For example, in Australia, using the Institute Multi-Purpose (IMP) model to study immigrants' incomes and expenditures, Hellwig et al. (1992) found that immigration brings about increases in GDP per capita. Similar conclusions have been reached using the ORANI model; see for example, Centre for International Economics (CIE) (1988).

Although most researchers who have examined the overall economic consequences of immigration have found evidence to suggest that immigration generates positive economic effects for the host country, a comprehensive view of the economic consequences of immigration requires the consideration of more specific results. The remainder of this section discusses some of these issues.

4.1.1   Labour Market Impact

Much of the literature on the economic impact of immigration, particularly in the US, Canada and Australia, examines the impact of immigration on the labour market of the host country. Two effects can be distinguished; these are an overall impact and partial effects on specific groups of native workers.

Tu (1991, p.156) argued that 'the groups of workers whose skills are complementary to those of immigrants will unambiguously experience an improvement of their position relative to the groups whose skills are substitutable for those of immigrants'. Borjas (1994a, 1995) and Borjas et al.

(1991, 1996) found that the inflow of less-skilled immigrants contributed to reduce the wages and employment rates of less skilled Americans, specifically of US high school dropouts during the 1980s, relative to those of more skilled American workers. Similarly, De New and Zimmermann (1993) concluded that blue collar immigrant workers in Germany negatively affect the wages of blue collar Germans and themselves on the whole. Razin and Sadka (1995) argued that with a malfunctioning labour market, particularly in those economies with less wage flexibility such as many of the countries in Western Europe, immigration exacerbates the imperfections in the market and reduce the share of the native-born population in the migration-induced domestic income.

However, distributional issues apart, researchers tend to be more positive than negative about the effects of immigration on the native labour market and national income. For example, because of production complementarities between immigrant workers and the stock of native productive inputs, Borjas (1994b, 1995) estimated that immigrant workers in the US generate an economic benefit of between $US6 billion and $US20 billion annually. He also argued that this benefit could be increased substantially if more skilled immigrants were attracted.

Studying the effects of immigration to Germany based on local labour markets data, Pischke and Velling (1994) found no detrimental effect of immigration. Similarly, examining the impact of immigration on the income of various groups of resident workers in the US and Europe, Gang and Rivera (1994) found that these effects were insignificant.

Another study by Friedberg and Hunt (1995), based on empirical analysis of several countries, estimated that a 1 per cent reduction in native wages would require at least a 10 per cent increase in the proportion of immigrants in the country's population. Friedberg and Hunt also argued that the potential for reductions in employment opportunities of native-born workers, even those who should be the closest substitutes with immigrant labour, was also insignificant.

Researchers have also found evidence that immigration can improve the efficiency of the host economy through the provision of workers with the skills and occupational mobility required by the changing needs of the host country economy. For example, Green (1995) examined the labour market experience of immigrants in Canada during the 1980s and found that immigrants, particularly those who are assessed on their skills to enter the country, are more occupationally mobile than workers born in Canada even after a substantial time in Canada. Green argued that immigration has improved the efficiency of the Canadian economy by contributing to a more flexible labour force. There is a role for immigration policy to shape the economic benefits from immigration by ensuring that the composition of the migrant intake reflects the needs of the host economy.

In Australia, two comprehensive accounts of the economic effects of immigration provided by Foster and Baker (1991) and by Wooden et al. (1994) reject the claim that immigration leads to increases in unemployment. There is also evidence that the level of skills of immigrants to Australia has been generally higher than the skills of the native workforce. However, there are concerns about the labour market performance among immigrants from a non-English-speaking background (NESB). In many cases non-English-speaking coincides with a refugee background.

Since the late 1980s NESB immigrants have received general recognition as one of the disadvantaged groups in Australian society. NESB immigrants are over-represented among the unemployed, the long-term unemployed and the underemployed. They are also over-represented in high-risk low-paid occupations in declining industries and fare relatively worse with respect to employment during recessions. Numerous studies have attributed this poor labour market performance to low levels of English proficiency. Stromback and Preston (1991) estimate that low proficiency in English costs the Australian economy $763 million annually in terms of output lost.

High levels of skills and educational qualifications do not traslate into equivalent occupation and earning status for NESB immigrants. Researchers have found that NESB immigrants workers employed in Australia exhibit a much higher incidence of over-education compared with workers from other backgrounds. For example, Flatau et al. (1995) show that 35 per cent of NESB employed workers in Australia had a level of education higher than the level required for the tasks actually performed. This compares with 12 per cent among employed workers born in Australia and 13 per cent among immigrants born in the main English-speaking countries (ESB). Similarly, relative pay deprivation and low employment income are highest among NESB groups of workers.

It has also been found that, notwithstanding the implementation of labour market programmes and other measures designed to improve the employability of NESB people, the labour market difficulties faced by NESB immigrants have increased during the 1990s. Thus, in comparing the labour market experience of NESB immigrants and workers born in Australia during the last three recessions, Brooks and Williams (1995) found that although during recessions NESB people experience lower participation and higher unemployment rates than persons born in Australia, the differences in these rates between those birthplaces were largest during the 1990-92 recession, and have persisted during the initial years of recovery. The same authors also found that even when the composition of the migration intake since 1990 has been inclined towards highly skilled people, males arriving since 1990 have also had an above-average concentration in the less skilled occupation group of labourers and related workers.

Studying the experience of NESB retrenchees in the Western region of Melbourne, Pearce et al. (1995) expressed concern about current labour market and training programs targeting NESB unemployed and the present and future impact of economic restructuring upon these people. They concluded that past experience suggest that NESB unemployed are among those who benefit least from programs; that the capacity of these programs to adequately cater to the needs of NESB people can still be questioned; that economic restructuring has hit particularly hard on NESB workers through high levels of retrenchment and the imposition of far more stringent demands on job applicants which might further disavantage those with low levels of English and literacy skills, making more difficult the search for re-employment for NESB retrenchees.

4.1.2   Other Economic Effects of Immigration

The effects of immigration on a number of macroeconomic variables have also
been studied. There have been analyses on the economies of scale associated
with immigration, on the impact of immigration on consumption, capital
stock, balance of payments, prices, government budgets, economic growth
and the environment.

Wooden *et al.* (1994) reviewed the literature on the economic effects of
immigration in Australia. He found that the contribution of immigration to
the Australian economy through economies of scale cannot be ignored, and
that immigration increases aggregate consumption per head. No evidence
has been found of any significant effect of immigration on either price or
wage inflation. Researchers have also failed to find evidence to support reductions in immigration as a measure to offset Australia's external deficits.
For example, Junankar *et al.* (1995) argued that, although net migration
seems to worsen the current account balance, immigrants do not have a significant impact on the current account balance. Moreover, simulation results
using macroeconomic models of the Australian economy suggest a positive
correlation between immigration and improvements in the current account
in the long run.

Concerning the impact of immigration on capital stock and investment,
the literature review conducted by Wooden *et al.* (1994) found that, although immigrants can bring funds with them and accumulate savings after
migrating, it is widely recognised that the amounts involved are insufficient
to meet the additional demand on capital requirements brought about by
immigration. Thus, since the existing capital stock must be spread over a
larger population, immigration has a capital-widening effect. Immigration
is expected to increase investment through affecting the rate of return to
capital. However, empirical studies on the impact of immigration on the
long-term investment to output ratio have produced mixed results.

The relationship between international movements of people and capital
has also been studied. Clarke (1995a, 1995b, 1995c), Clarke and Martin
(1995) and Clarke and Smith (1995), used data for the UK, Australia, Canada

and the US for the period 1870 to 1991. They suggested that important linkages between capital and labour movements exist; more specifically, it was found that 'capital chased labour' in all three labour immigration economies. This outcome was found to be particularly strong for Australia and Canada over the complete sample period.

There has also been debate about the relationship between immigration, as an important source of population growth in Australia, and the environment. It is estimated that since 1945, net migration has contributed about 40 per cent to Australia's population growth and will take over from natural increase as the most important component of population growth next century; see ABS (1996b). Issues such as optimal population, congestion, pollution, waste management, overcrowding, water supply, agricultural land degradation, the destruction of wilderness areas and resource depletion have been discussed.

The debate is polarised between those, particularly biologists and environmentalists, who oppose immigration in order to stop environmental degradation, and those who argue that environmental problems cannot be properly addressed through population policies. The latter group argue that problems need to be addressed directly through better management or the use of efficient pricing mechanisms to take proper account of the environmental costs involved in any development strategy; see, for example, Clarke et al. (1990), Clarke and Ng (1993, 1995) and Clarke (1995d). Detailed arguments in the debate on population and the environment are presented by Harding (1995).

Wooden et al. (1994, p.25) concluded that 'the evidence inclines us to be more positive than negative about the economic impact of immigration'. A similar conclusion was reached in an earlier study by Foster and Baker (1991, p.130) who suggested that 'while the economic case in favour of immigration might be marginal, the economic case against would appear even weaker. Four main reasons are cited in support of this position - the lack of influence of immigration on aggregate unemployment; the apparent margin of skill in favour of immigrant workers; immigration's stimulus to the building industry; and the likely positive effect on general living standards'.

4.1.3   Impact of Immigration on Government Budgets

The budgetary implications of immigration have also been the subject of considerable research. Empirical studies on this area in several countries present mixed results. However, a majority of them tend to be more positive than negative about the budgetary implications of immigration. For example, a survey of empirical research on the distributional effects of public transfers between immigrants and natives in high immigration countries, conducted by Weber and Straubhaar (1994), showed that 4 out of 17 studies reviewed found negative transfer effects for natives, whereas 6 of the studies concluded that immigration generated positive transfer effects for the host countries natives. Based on the 1990 Swiss Consumer Survey, Weber and Straubhaar (1994, p.25) found 'an average financial gain (through the government budget) for the Swiss population of around $1,700 per foreign resident household'.

In Australia, three reports commissioned by the former Bureau of Immigration and Population Research (BIPR) on the effects of immigration on Commonwealth, State and Local government budgets, and conducted by the CIE (1992), Mathews (1992) and Cutts (1992), found no evidence of a negative budgetary effect of immigration. However, Mathews and Cutts note that their results should be qualified by the fact they are based on actual expenditure not on what should be provided by the State and Local governments to meet the needs of some migrant groups.

Using generational accounting methodology, Ablett (1994, p.25) concluded that 'results suggest that future migrants belonging to cohorts alive in 1990/91 would, under the assumption of unchanged fiscal policies, contribute in a significant net positive way to the Australian public sector over their remaining lifetimes. This result is driven by the relative dominance of young working aged people in the composition of migrant intakes, compared to the resident Australian population'. A study by Meikle and Tulpule (1985) also highlighted the positive budgetary implications associated with the age composition of the migrant intake. However, Ablett (1994) also found evidence to suggest that future migration *per se* may have a net negative, though small, effect on the public sector.

Some researchers argue that the potential for a negative impact of immigration on government budgets is higher in countries with labour market imperfections and generous welfare programs; see, for example Razin and Sadka (1995) and LaLonde and Topel (1994). Studying the welfare recipiency of immigrants to the US, Borjas and Trejo (1993) argued that over two-thirds of the variance of welfare recipiency among immigrant groups in the US are explained by a few source country characteristics. Borjas (1994c) and Borjas and Hilton (1995) found that 21 per cent of immigrant households receive welfare assistance compared with 14 per cent of native American households, and that immigrant participation in welfare programmes is on the rise in the US.

Further discussion of the impact of immigration on government expenditure in Australia is presented in chapter 6.

4.2 Other Immigration Issues

Cultural, political, social, demographic and spatial aspects associated with immigration have also attracted the attention of researchers. Chiswick (1992) edited a collection of reports on different aspects of immigration, language and ethnicity in the US and Canada. Campos and Lien (1995) and Bratsberg (1995) have examined legal and illegal immigration to the US and the linkages between these immigration flows and source countries characteristics. A historical study of ethnic politics among specific immigrant groups in the US was made by Gutierrez (1995), who examined the case of Mexican Americans and Mexican immigrants. Massey (1995) studied the changes in the nature of ethnicity in the US as a result of new immigration waves. Lazear (1995) discussed the welfare implications of policies which encourage assimilation compared with policies which encourage multiculturalism, particularly in terms of minority groups learning the native language of the host country.

In Australia, the book edited by Jupp and Kabala (1993) discussed several issues on the politics of Australian immigration. A broader range of immigration issues was presented in Wooden et al. (1994) who included sections on demographic and spatial aspects, social issues, immigration policy and the economic consequences of immigration.

Although the range of issues associated with immigration is quite large, this section focuses on two aspects which are most relevant for this book: these are the demographic role of immigration and the implications of immigrants' country of origin.

4.2.1   The Demographic Role of Immigration

International migration plays a role in the process of population ageing. As discussed in chapter 2, demographic transitions are not due only to a country's internal developments. Migration provides a mechanism for relieving population pressures. Through international migration and the selectivity of the migration process, demographic changes diffuse from country to country. The demographic impact of migration on the country of origin and on the country of destination depends on the size of the movement of people, the migrant's age structure, and their mortality and fertility characteristics.

Immigration can slow down the extent of population ageing in the destination country. However, researchers have highlighted the limits of this retarding of the ageing effect achievable through immigration. Young (1990) and Schmertmann (1992) argued that immigration, as a means to retarding population ageing, is an inferior mechanism compared with fertility increases. For example, Young (1990, p.20) concluded that 'increasing the level of fertility is a more efficient way of retarding the ageing of the population than increasing the level of immigration, because the same effect on the proportion aged 65 years or more would be achieved through a smaller increase in population'. It is important to note that the term 'efficient' as used by Young is strictly limited to the demographic context explained by her. A broader definition of efficiency including, for example, costs of child rearing and early education, might produce different results. In the case of migrants, child rearing and early education represent a net saving for the host country and a loss for the country where the child rearing and eduction occurred, which increases with the level of qualification attained before migrating.

Immigration adds to the future cohorts of elderly people. As immigrants arrive as young adults, their share in the elderly population of the host country grows faster than that of natives. In Australia, it is estimated that the overseas-born elderly population grew three times as fast as the elderly who were born in Australia in the 1980s, with the elderly from non-English speaking backgrounds growing more than four times as fast as the the elderly who were born in Australia during the same years; see Hugo (1994).

There also exist practical limits to the use of immigration as an effective measure to offset falls in the size of the workforce. For example, the OECD (1995, p.41) estimated that the number of working-age immigrants needed in 2050 to offset fully the fall in working-age population between 2000 and 2050 (when the working population stabilises at a lower level) would be around 13 to 15 million for each of Japan, Germany and Italy. This amounts to between 20 and 40 per cent of the working-age population.

Immigration is not a perfect substitute for fertility. However, immigration does slow down the extent of population ageing in the destination country. In fact, immigration has contributed to make Australia's population one of the youngest among Western countries; see National Population Council (NPC) (1991, p.4). This retarding of the ageing effect due to immigration stems not only from the fact that the immigrant intakes exhibit an age structure younger than the native population. Fertility and mortality differentials between immigrants and the native-born persons can also influence the patterns of fertility and mortality in the host country, especially in countries where immigrants represent a significant proportion of the total population. Lower mortality and higher fertility rates among immigrant groups compared with the native population have been well documented in the case of Australia; see Hugo (1994). These issues are discussed further in chapter 5.

4.2.2 Implications of Immigrants' Country of Origin

A successful immigration experience, in terms of the economic success of immigrants in the destination country, has been linked to the national origin of immigrants. Research on this issue has been conducted both overseas and in Australia. Overseas studies include those conducted by Borjas (1987,

1991, 1992), Borjas and Freeman (1992), Funkhouser and Trejo (1993), and McDowell and Singell (1993). A comprehensive review of Australian studies is presented in Wooden *et al.* (1994).

Borjas (1987) found that observed differences in the US earnings of immigrants with the same measured skills but from different home countries can be attributable to variations in the characteristics of immigrants' countries of origin at the time of migration. He found that economic and political characteristics of the countries of origin at the time of migration explain much of the economic success or failure of immigrants in the US. Using data on the earnings of immigrants from 41 different countries from the 1970 and 1980 censuses, Borjas (1987, p.552) found that persons from Western European countries have done well in the US and have experienced a general increase in earnings relative to their measured skills over the postwar period. On the other hand, persons from less developed countries have not performed well and have exhibited a general decrease in earnings over the postwar period.

Studying the point system of immigration used in Canada, Borjas (1991) argued that the point system 'works' because it alters the national origin mix of the immigrant intake. National origin seems to be important not only to explain the performance of first generation migrants but also the economic success or failure of second generations. Borjas (1992) found that the earnings of second generation Americans are strongly influenced by variables describing the economic conditions in the source countries of their parents.

In Australia, researchers have studied the implications of immigrants' country of origin in regard to three main indicators of labour market achievement, employment status, earnings, and occupational attainment. The general conclusion is that immigrants from non-English-speaking backgrounds do worse than both the native-born and immigrants born in English-speaking countries.

The lack of proficiency in the English language seems to explain much of immigrants' difficulty in the labour market. Poor English language ability among immigrant males is associated with a probability of unemployment double that of an otherwise comparable group, according to Inglis and Stromback (1988). The unemployment probabilities are over three times that for the control group according to Brooks and Volker (1985), and even larger according to Wooden and Robertson (1989). Stromback (1988) has also found that lack of English proficiency reduces earnings among immigrants by about 10 per cent; see also Wooden *et al.* (1994).

After English proficiency, length of residence in Australia accounts for significant differences in labour market outcomes among immigrants, particularly in terms of employment status of those born in countries where English is not the main language. According to Inglis and Stromback (1986), the difference in the probability of unemployment between the least employable birthplace group of migrant males and a comparable group of Australian-born males decreases from about 20 percentage points on arrival to about 5 percentage points after 5 years of living in Australia. Other studies on the implications of length of residence on the employability of NESB migrants report even more favourable results than those presented by Inglis and Stromback; see, for example, Wooden and Robertson (1989).

Migration category has also been found to play an important role in labour market outcomes. Refugees are found to be the most disadvantaged in the labour market, although much of their disadvantage can be explained by the lack of English language proficiency and recent arrival. Wooden and Robertson (1989) estimate the probability of unemployment for Asian refugees who arrived between 1983 and 1987 at 20 to 30 percentage points higher than other entry categories.

Difficulties in the transferability of skills of immigrants to the Australian labour market are found to contribute to observed differences in earnings and occupational attainment between otherwise comparable groups of people with similar levels of education. This in turn, it is argued, reflects differences in the quality of education. Country-specific skills are more difficult to transfer and increase with level of education, so the relative income advantage of natives increases as the level of education increases; see Beggs and Chapman (1988a), and Wooden *et al.* (1994).

4.2.3   Immigration and Ethnicity

Language, religious and cultural factors are commonly associated with the concept of 'ethnicity'. Ethnic characteristics remain with individuals throughout their lives, and their importance tends to increase as people get older, even in the case of immigrants who have spent most of their lives in the host country; see Rowland (1991b). Ethnicity provides a basis for a continuity of life patterns, which plays a central role for a succesful adjustment to and well-being in old age.

Like many other social concepts, there is not a universally accepted definition of ethnicity. The range of approaches to ethnicity goes from broad classical definitions which define an ethnic group as 'any group of individuals with a shared sense of peoplehood based on race, religion, or national origin' (Barresi and Stull 1993, p.6), to narrower approaches that tend to identify ethnicity with minority status. Some approaches lean more heavily on self-identification, which, it is argued, gives the group a social force through the willingness to participate in the fate of the group. Conversely, some definitions rely more on historical ancestry, which offers the advantage of providing more measurable information. Rowland (1991b, p.9) noted that, in a country like Australia, this type of definition 'could easily exclude Australian ethnicity since all Australians, apart from the Aborigines, are of immigrant origin'; and assuming that people identify with their ancestors' country of origin, this approach denies the possibility of any process of assimilation of immigrants and their descendants. Nonetheless, the lack of a clear and generally acceptable definition of ethnicity led to the inclusion of an ancestry question in the 1986 Australian Census as the most practical method of collecting information on ethnicity.

The lack of a consensus among social scientists on defining ethnicity does not preclude the existence of a popular notion of the term. Thus, for example, in the US the term 'ethnic' is usually assigned to 'non-white' minorities. In Australia, migrant groups whose members' first spoken language is other than English are referred to as 'ethnic communities'. The term covers second and later generations.

This book does not undertake an analysis of the ethnic characteristics of Australia's immigrants; rather, in allowing for a certain amount of population heterogeneity the emphasis is on immigrants' country of origin. Specifically, the distinction used is between immigrants from non-English-speaking backgrounds and their descendants, and Australians born in the main English-speaking countries as defined by the Australian Bureau of Statistics (ABS). The main English-speaking countries group includes people born in Australia, UK and Ireland, New Zealand, Canada, the US, and South Africa. The rationale for this distinction stems from the differences in social and economic characteristics exhibited by these population groups, as discussed in Part III of this book. However, it is useful to review the main theoretical arguments about ethnicity, particularly those regarding the relationship between ethnicity and ageing.

According to Rowland (1991b), the theoretical development of the ethnic aged is still in its first stages and has predominantly originated in the US. Therefore, the explanatory power of the theory is restricted when applied to Australia. Although ethnic communities are ageing more rapidly than the native population, most Australian studies on the ethnic aged are empirical and use birthplace as a measure of ethnicity. The work of Price (1989, 1993), who used a broader approach to ethnicity, is an exemption.

The two more relevant theoretical developments about the ethnic aged are the 'modernisation theory' and the 'double jeopardy hypothesis'. According to Cowgill's (1974, 1986) modernisation hypothesis, the process of modernisation, such as that experienced by rural-urban migrants or first-generation settlers from less developed countries, through the abandonment of extended family households in favour of nuclear family units, brings about the loss of social status of the elderly. Rowland (1991b, p.11), in summarising the criticisms of the modernisation theory, stated that the theory 'fails to differentiate between ethnic groups and assumes that modern families are unsupportive of the aged'.

Although not without reservations, the 'double jeopardy hypothesis' is more widely accepted. This theory states that elderly ethnics are more socially disadvantaged than elderly members of the majority population: 'occupying two stigmatised statuses is accompanied by more negative consequences than occupying either status alone. The expectation is that being old and a member of a disadvantaged ethnic group has more adverse effects than being younger, or being an older member of the majority population'; see Rowland (1991b, p.12). The main criticism of this hypothesis is that double jeopardy can also be used to explain sources of variation other than ethnicity and age, and one could even talk about 'multiple jeopardy'. In addition, there exists some evidence in support of the contradictory hypothesis that ageing appears to diminish social and economic differences between ethnic and cultural groupings, that is, the 'age-as-leveller' hypothesis; see Rowland (1991b, p.12).

The adaptation of immigrants to the recipient country is usually a life-long process, whose difficulty increases with the migrant's age. People who migrate at older ages face more difficulties integrating into community and family life than younger migrants. But even immigrants who have spent many years in the recipient country experience a psychological reversion to their country of birth customs at older ages; see Boyer (1987, p.109). Adaptation is obviously made more difficult as the cultural gap between the home country and that of settlement increases, particularly when there exist language differences. The sharing of language, religion, history, cultural traditions, geographic origin, and other factors, that leads to the constitution of nations, also provides a basis for immigrants to form distinct communities within the recipient country, that is ethnic communities. It is within this context that the concept of ethnicity acquires more relevance. Ethnicity is a fact of life in major immigrant recipient countries. Ethnic characteristics accompany individuals throughout their lives, and there is increasing evidence that their importance rises with age, providing a source of identity, strength and group membership in later life.

Part III

Population Decomposition

Chapter 5

Demographic Characteristics

It was suggested in chapter 4 that although immigration is not a perfect substitute for fertility, immigration does slow down the extent of population ageing in the destination country. In effect, immigration has contributed to make Australia's population one of the youngest among the industrialised countries.

The extent of the retarding of the ageing effect due to immigration depends on the age structure, fertility and mortality characteristics of immigrants. Immigrants, characterised by higher fertility, lower mortality and a younger age structure compared with the native-born population, have the potential to slow down the extent of population ageing in the destination country.

This chapter discusses the demographic characteristics of the Australian population and of the people migrating to Australia. Section 5.1 focuses on the size and age structure of the Australian population. For purposes of comparison, the Australian population is classified according to country of birth in three groups: people born in Australia; people born overseas in countries with an English-speaking background or ESB, which include people born in the UK and Ireland, New Zealand, Canada, the US, and South Africa; and people born in countries with a non-English-speaking background or NESB, which include immigrants born in countries other than the English-speaking countries listed above. This birthplace classification is retained throughout this study. In Part IV, this classification is extended to include second and later generations.

Section 5.2 examines the determinants of population change, namely, net migration flows, fertility and mortality. A comparison of these demographic characteristics using the birthplace classification mentioned above is undertaken.

5.1   Size and Age Structure of the Population

The number of overseas-born reached 4.034 million people, or 22.8 per cent of the total Australian population, in June 1993 (ABS 1994a). This increase, from the 20.6 per cent overseas-born in 1981, has been due to the high levels of immigration experienced particularly during the second half of the 1980s. Almost 60 per cent of immigrants residing in Australia in 1993 were born in non-English-speaking background countries, and over the 10 years 1983-93 more than 50 per cent of new arrivals came from Asia; the four countries Hong Kong, Viet Nam, the Philippines and Malaysia contributed 26 per cent of settler arrivals between 1988 and 1992 (ABS 1994b, p.10).

According to the 1991 Census, 75 per cent of the Australian population were of English-speaking background and 18 per cent were either born in or had parents who were both born in a non-English-speaking country. The percentage of the population over 5 years of age speaking a language other than English at home increased from 14 to 17 per cent between 1986 and 1991; see Shu *et al.* (1994, pp.64-67).

The Australian population has displayed a certain amount of ageing over the last 20 or so years. For example, the proportion of people aged 65 years and over increased from 8.5 per cent of the total population in 1972 to 12 per cent in 1993; see Shu *et al.* (1994, p.8). An initial idea of the age structure of the population and its composition is shown in Table 5.1, which refers to 1993, and gives the percentages in each age group. The table is based on calculations using ABS (1994a) data stored on magnetic media. Some of the rows do not add to 100 due to rounding. In this table, individuals are distinguished by their place of birth, so that many of those who are listed as being born in Australia have parents, or grandparents, who were born overseas. By

Table 5.1: Population Age Structure by Sex, Age and Birthplace, 1993

	0-4	5-14	15-24	25-54	55-64	65+	Total (000s)
Australia							
Males	10	18	18	39	7	9	6,754.15
Females	9	16	17	38	7	12	6,873.81
Total	9	17	17	39	7	11	13,627.96
Overseas							
Males	1	6	10	56	13	14	2,043.28
Females	1	5	10	56	12	16	1,990.23
Total	1	6	10	56	13	15	4,033.51
ESB							
Males	1	5	9	58	12	15	831.89
Females	1	5	9	56	11	19	813.48
Total	1	5	9	57	12	17	1,645.37
NESB							
Males	1	6	11	55	14	13	1,211.39
Females	1	6	11	56	12	14	1,176.76
Total	1	6	11	55	13	13	2,388.15
ALL							
Males	8	15	16	43	8	10	8,797.42
Females	7	14	15	42	8	13	8,864.05
Total	7	14	16	43	8	12	17,661.47

definition, immigrants are not born in Australia and hence far fewer immigrants are children, compared with the native-born population. Thus, at any time the stock of immigrants is much older than the native-born population. The flows of migrants, however, are much younger than the native population and this has important demographic implications as discussed below. To the extent that relevant demographic and socio-economic characteristics of individuals are influenced by the background of their parents, as well as their own country of birth, then the birthplace grouping used in Table 5.1 may conceal useful information about the demographic impact of immigration.

Information relating to the age structure of those who were born overseas, and that of later generations, has been assembled by Kee (1992, pp.27-31), and is summarised in Table 5.2. In this table, the term 'second generation' is used to describe the children of immigrants.

Table 5.2: Age Structure of Immigrants and Later Generations

Generation	0-4	5-14	15-24	25-54	55-64	65+
All	7.6	15.7	16.6	40.3	9.2	10.5
Immigrant + 2nd Generation	4.0	11.6	16.1	46.3	10.9	11.1
3rd and Later Generations	8.4	16.4	16.8	39.4	8.6	10.3

5.2   Determinants of Population Change

Changes in the size and structure of the population are a result of changes in migration, mortality and fertility rates. These aspects of population change and their differences according to the birthplace of the population components are discussed below.

5.2.1   Net Migration Flows

Population ageing is likely to continue, as discussed in detail below, particularly during the second and third decades of the 21st century. However, population ageing in Australia is less than in most industrialised countries, mainly because of the higher levels of immigration. This is largely because immigrants are typically younger than the average population. In order to illustrate this feature, Table 5.3, based on calculations using Department of Immigration and Ethnic Affairs (DIEA) (1994) data, shows the age distribution of the annual net migration flows during the period 1989 to 1993 by sex and birthplace. Net migration is the difference between settler arrivals and permanent departures. This table shows that the Australian resident population has been augmented by net annual immigration flows of people with a relatively younger age structure. Furthermore, it can be seen that during the years covered by the table, migrants born in English-speaking background countries were slightly more concentrated at the base of the age pyramid, while those born in non-English-speaking background countries were more likely to migrate in their prime working age.

Table 5.3: Age Distribution of Net Migration Flows: Annual Average 1988/89-1992/93

	Percentages aged					
	0-4	5-14	15-24	25-54	55-64	65+
ESB Males	10.6	18.3	18.9	47.0	2.0	3.1
Females	11.7	20.3	17.1	41.3	4.9	4.6
Total	11.1	19.2	18.1	44.4	3.3	3.8
NESB Males	10.9	18.7	15.2	50.2	3.3	1.7
Females	9.7	16.2	18.8	49.4	4.0	2.0
Total	10.3	17.4	17.0	49.8	3.7	1.9
All Males	10.8	18.6	15.9	49.6	3.1	2.0
Females	10.0	16.8	18.5	48.2	4.1	2.4
Total	10.4	17.7	17.2	48.9	3.6	2.2

5.2.2 Fertility

Immigration may also contribute to slowing down the extent of population ageing if the fertility rates of immigrants are relatively higher than the fertility rates of the native population. Demographic differences between immigrants and the native population are indeed observed in terms of fertility rates as measured by total confinement rates. These rates are usually measured as the total number of children that 1,000 women bear over their lifetimes. Table 5.4, based on ABS (1994c, pp.44-45), shows that overseas-born women, particularly those from non-English-speaking backgrounds, experience fertility rates higher than women born in Australia. According to the 1991 birth rates and resident population, NESB women had a total confinement rate 8 per cent higher than those born in Australia and ESB women. Among the more fertile birthplace groups are those coming from Oceania, the Middle East and North Africa as well as from some Asian countries.

5.2.3 Mortality

The available evidence suggests that there are differences between the mortality rates of the various population groups. Information relating to death rates by birthplace in 1991 is given in Table 5.5, from ABS (1994c, pp.115-116), and shows that in 1991, overseas-born people had mortality rates lower

Table 5.4: Confinements per 1,000 Females by Birthplace of Mother, 1991

Birthplace of mother	15-19	20-24	25-29	30-34	35-39	40+	Total
Australia	22.3	72.7	130.7	98.5	32.8	4.7	1,809
Overseas	19.3	80.7	130.8	99.2	40.8	7.0	1,889
ESB	21.3	75.0	124.2	96.8	37.4	6.2	1,805
NESB	18.1	84.7	136.4	101.0	43.0	7.4	1,953
Oceania	30.9	89.5	128.5	107.3	46.1	8.3	2,053
Europe & USSR	19.0	84.1	127.9	85.9	31.9	5.2	1,770
Middle E & N Africa	78.8	185.2	173.8	110.7	56.3	11.3	3,076
Southeast Asia	9.7	55.9	120.8	106.4	59.5	14.5	1,834
Northeast Asia	1.2	29.4	144.0	113.5	43.6	6.6	1,691
Southern Asia	8.6	78.9	139.5	108.0	48.0	7.1	1,951
The Americas	12.9	60.8	123.0	111.8	45.9	9.4	1,894

than those of persons born in Australia. It also shows that NESB immigrants had lower rates than ESB immigrants in all age groups except males aged 45-54, for which the rate for NESB migrants was higher, and females aged 25-44, where the rates were equal.

The above comparison of demographic characteristics of migrants with those of the native-born population shows that the latter has been augmented by a migration intake with a younger age structure, and higher fertility and lower mortality rates. In view of the fact that the age structure is not very sensitive to changes in mortality, the net effect of immigration is therefore to reduce the extent of population ageing. Among the overseas-born Australians, the demographic characteristics of those born in non-English-speaking background countries appear to have a higher potential to slow population ageing.

As noted above, altering the age structure of the population is only one of the ways in which migration may affect social expenditure. In assessing the impact on social expenditure, account should also be taken of the social and economic characteristics of migrants. Socio-economic factors may either reinforce or offset the effects of the age structure. Some of the social and economic factors that are relevant when analysing the impact of migration on social expenditure are considered in the next chapter.

Table 5.5: Age-Specific Death Rates by Birthplace, 1991: Deaths per 1,000

Birthplace	0-14	15-24	25-44	45-54	55-64	65-74	75 +
Males							
Australia	0.8	1.1	1.6	4.4	13.0	31.8	93.1
Overseas	0.2	1.0	1.3	3.4	10.2	28.1	89.4
ESB	-	1.1	1.4	3.4	10.9	30.9	97.8
NESB	0.3	0.9	1.2	3.6	10.4	27.5	84.4
Females							
Australia	0.6	0.4	0.8	2.6	6.9	17.3	68.7
Overseas	0.2	0.4	0.6	2.0	5.4	15.5	67.2
ESB	-	0.4	0.6	2.2	6.1	17.4	72.8
NESB	0.3	0.3	0.6	1.9	5.1	14.6	63.7

Chapter 6

Socio-Economic Characteristics

This chapter examines the socio-economic differences between the birthplace groups of the Australian population which may be thought to be relevant in explaining the changes over time in expenditure within the social expenditure categories considered in this study. Social expenditure considered in this book consists of those items of government expenditure, including both Commonwealth and State governments' social expenditure which vary with age. These are aged pensions, other aged assistance, unemployment benefits, other social security benefits, health, education and employment. In chapter 4 it was argued that a successful immigration experience, particularly in terms of the economic success of immigrants in the destination country, is linked to the national origin of immigrants. Place of birth influences several socio-economic indicators which, in turn, affect government social expenditure.

To the extent that there are significant differences between birthplace groups, studies which have treated all residents as homogeneous may have been misleading. The wide variety of ethnic groups and countries of origin of immigrants suggests that there may indeed be differences in social and economic characteristics among overseas-born, and between them and people born in Australia. Section 6.1 discusses these differences. Several socio-economic indicators are examined. Particular attention is paid to the dependency upon social security pensions and benefits, labour force status, education and health. Section 6.2 examines the issue of whether there exists

an adjustment process through which the social and economic characteristics
of different population groups tend to converge.

6.1   Factors Affecting Social Expenditure

It is known that ESB immigrants tend to be better off in terms of employment
prospects and income than those from a non-English-speaking background;
see Wooden (1990), Johnson (1991) and Ackland and Williams (1992). Family sponsored migrants are characterised by low participation rates in the
workforce and high unemployment. Refugees are generally relatively young,
but almost all of them come from non-English-speaking countries and their
unemployment rate is one of the highest among overseas-born. These socio-
economic differences between birthplace groups of the Australian population
lead to differences in the associated social expenditure costs. The main factors involved are discussed below.

6.1.1   Social Security Pensions

Social security pensions in Australia are means-tested, so that economic status influences their receipt. Table 6.1 shows rates per 1,000 population of
the same birthplace receiving different types of social security pension, using data from the Department of Social Security (DSS) (1995a). These are
the age pension, disability pension, widow's pension, mature age pension
and sole parent pension. Overseas-born people, particularly those born in
non-English-speaking countries, present the highest rates of people receiving
social security pensions, especially age and disability pensions. However, the
data shown in Table 6.1 give only a partial indication of differences in the
propensity to receive means-tested pensions because of the differences in age
structure.

6.1.2   Labour Force Status

Social expenditure on unemployment benefits and employment programs are
of course directly affected by labour force status. Being a long-term unem-

Table 6.1: People Receiving Social Security Pensions by Type of Pension and Birthplace: June 1995 (Rates per 1.000 population of same birthplace)

Birthplace	Age Pen	Disabil	Widow	Mature	Sole P	Total
Australia	79.5	30.4	2.1	2.4	19.2	133.7
Overseas	132.4	47.6	6.4	5.3	15.7	207.4
ESB	124.6	30.8	4.9	5.3	17.3	182.9
NESB	137.8	59.2	7.4	5.2	14.6	224.2
Europe	230.2	86.1	7.7	7.5	9.9	341.5
Middle East	82.8	117.8	8.6	4.0	27.8	241.1
America	41.9	38.8	7.6	3.2	26.4	117.8
Africa	108.2	47.3	7.4	4.8	17.0	184.7
Asia	39.5	15.7	7.0	2.8	15.2	80.3
Oceania	25.1	23.0	4.0	1.2	32.1	85.4

Table 6.2: Unemployment Rates by Birthplace: August 1993 (percentages)

Birthplace	Unemployment Rate	Long-term Rate
Australia	10.0	3.4
Overseas	13.1	5.4
ESB	9.2	2.9
NESB	16.0	7.3

ployed person is a prerequisite to be eligible for most employment programs. As can be seen from Table 6.2, from ABS (1994d, p.23), which shows unemployment and long-term unemployment rates by birthplace of the Australian population, both rates are highest among the overseas-born compared with people born in Australia. Rates for those born in non-English-speaking countries are higher than for those born in the main English-speaking countries.

Although the employability of people with higher educational levels is higher than those without post-school qualifications for all birthplace groups, unemployment rates among qualified people present a pattern by birthplace similar to that shown in Table 6.2; see ABS (1994d, p.26).

There are also significant differences in employment experience among NESB groups. For instance, in August 1993, people in Australia who were born in Italy experienced an unemployment rate of 8.2 per cent, whereas those born in Lebanon and Vietnam experienced rates of 37.5 and 31.9 per

Table 6.3: People Receiving Social Security Benefits: May 1995 (per 1,000)

Birthplace	Unempl	Sickness	Spec Ben	Total
Australia	44.3	2.5	0.4	47.2
Overseas	46.9	2.8	3.7	53.4
ESB	37.2	2.7	0.5	40.4
NESB	53.6	2.9	5.9	62.4
Europe	37.7	3.1	1.8	42.7
Middle East	120.9	6.8	8.7	136.4
America	70.2	3.5	6.9	80.6
Africa	56.9	3.1	6.2	66.2
Asia	60.3	1.7	11.0	73.0
Oceania	60.8	3.1	7.6	71.5

cent respectively; see ABS (1994d, p.23). As mentioned above, these differences reflect a number of factors, such as length of residence in Australia and category of arrival. The importance of the time period since arrival in the employability of immigrants, particularly NESB migrants, with respect to the time it takes to learn English and to acquire labour market knowledge, has been widely recognised. The unemployment rate of NESB migrants who arrived between 1991 and August 1993 was 45.1 per cent, but it was 19 per cent for those who arrived during the decade of the 1980s; see ABS (1994d, p.25). Similarly, the long-term unemployment rate halved for the latter group.

The fact that NESB immigrants experience high rates of unemployment is also shown in Table 6.3, from DSS (1995a), which shows rates per thousand of population receiving social security benefits by type of benefit and birthplace. It can be seen from this table that 62.4 per thousand NESB people receive Social Security benefits, particularly Unemployment Benefits, compared with 47.2 per thousand of those born in Australia and an even lower rate for ESB migrants.

Migration category is also an important influence in the labour force status of the overseas-born population. Among principal applicant immigrants aged 18 and over who arrived in Australia after 1970 and before September 1993, refugees experienced an unemployment rate of 18.3 per cent, which was similar to that of family sponsored migrants. Unsponsored migrants experienced a rate of 11.8 per cent, while not surprisingly the lowest rate corresponded to immigrants sponsored by an employer; see ABS (1994e, p.6). Accordingly, among the above mentioned principal applicant immigrants, 32.5 per cent of refugees and 31 per cent of family sponsored immigrants declared a government pension or cash benefit as the main source of income at September 1993, compared with 19.7 per cent among unsponsored immigrants, with the lowest rate corresponding to employer sponsored immigrants; see ABS (1994e, p.10).

Notwithstanding the high unemployment rates experienced by overseas-born people, their participation in employment programs appears to be very low. This is especially true of NESB people. As an illustration, the Survey of Training and Education (conducted by the ABS during April and May 1993) shows that of those unemployed in Australia, 57 per cent of people born in Australia, 48 per cent of ESB people and 37 per cent of NESB people had undertaken some training during the 12 months prior to interview; see ABS (1994f, p.14).

6.1.3 Educational Attainment

Immigrants tend to be better educated than people born in Australia. According to the 1991 Census, of those aged 15 years or more, 9.8 per cent of those born in Australia had attained a degree or higher, compared with 12.9 per cent of overseas-born. Among the latter group, 12.8 per cent of ESB migrants and 13.2 per cent of NESB immigrants had a degree or higher; see ABS (1994b, p.95). The skills and qualifications of immigrants is often regarded as one of the main economic benefits generated by immigration; see, for example, Foster and Baker (1991).

Since the majority of immigrants arrive in Australia as adults, having completed schooling in their birthplace, education expenditure on immigrants is expected to be lower than on people born in Australia. However, a significant proportion of overseas-born people obtain post-school qualifications in Australia, as shown in Table 6.4, which is based on ABS, *Survey of Education and Training* (1993b), data stored on magnetic media. The figures include

Table 6.4: Percentage of People with Australian Post-School Qualification by Birthplace and Age

Age Group	Australia-born	Overseas-born	ESB	NESB
15-24	28.1	22.0	19.9	23.8
25-29	48.8	32.2	32.6	31.8
30-34	50.8	31.9	36.2	28.6
35-39	53.1	29.4	35.9	24.9
40-44	50.8	30.4	34.8	26.8
45-49	47.4	24.8	27.6	22.4
50-54	48.9	23.7	27.4	20.7
55-64	43.8	18.0	21.1	15.6
Total	44.3	27.1	30.2	24.6

immigrants who obtained an Australian qualification prior to immigration.

A study of the educational achievements and aspirations of birthplace groups in New South Wales concluded that young people born in some of the main non-English-speaking countries, particularly in East and Southeast Asia, achieved much higher participation rates in higher education during 1994 than those born in Australia and those born in some of the main English-speaking countries, such as the UK, Ireland and New Zealand. The same study also concluded that educational aspirations of Year 11 school students born in the same Asian countries are much higher than those born in Australia, New Zealand, the UK, and Ireland; see Parr and Mok (1995, pp.1-8).

Studies have shown that immigrants who receive Australian education perform much better in the labour market compared with immigrants with no Australian schooling or with qualifications obtained overseas; see, for example, Chapman and Salvage (1994) and Will (1996). According to Will (1996, p.1), Australian education is associated with higher returns to both total education and workforce experience. Furthermore, he suggested that returns to Australian education increase with the amount received and that pre-tertiary Australian education is important.

However, the majority of immigrants completed most of their schooling overseas, so education expenditure on immigrants is lower than that on

Table 6.5: Per Capita Education Expenditure: 1989-90

Level of Education	Australia	Overseas	ESB	NESB	Total
Pre-schools	20	4	4	4	17
Primary	339	122	91	146	291
Secondary	317	146	123	163	279
TAFE	83	109	100	116	89
Other	76	94	71	110	80
Total	836	475	389	539	756

people born in Australia. This is illustrated in Table 6.5, from Mathews (1992, p.87), which shows per capita education expenditure by country of birth funded by Australian state governments, excluding university education costs. This table shows that per capita education expenditure on people born in Australia is higher than that on overseas-born. Among the latter, NESB people appear to use education services more intensively than their ESB counterparts. Differences in per capita expenditure between persons born in Australia and those born overseas decrease with the level of education. At Technical and Further Education (TAFE) level, expenditure on those born overseas, particularly on NESB people, is higher than on persons born in Australia.

6.1.4 Health

Immigrants, particularly NESB people, appear to be less affected by illness than persons born in Australia. Using an indirect standardisation method on data collected from the 1989-90 National Health Survey, the ABS (1994c, pp.93-98) estimated that 66.4 per cent of males born in Australia reported a recent illness, compared with 65.4 per cent of ESB males and 55.9 per cent of NESB males. Similar results were found for females. In the case of long-term illness, ESB females reported higher rates than females born in Australia and NESB females. NESB males reported slightly lower rates for long-term illness than males born in Australia. When reporting mental disorder, NESB people reported higher rates than ESB and persons born in Australia; see also Minas *et al.* (1996).

In terms of health risk factors, the same ABS study (1994c, pp.98-103) found that NESB people exhibit lower alcohol and cigarette consumption than both ESB and people born in Australia. However, a higher proportion of NESB people are overweight and exercise less than their counterparts born in Australia and in other English-speaking countries.

In addition, several studies have argued that NESB people tend to find their first jobs in occupations where they are at the greatest risk of injury and accidents and, therefore, chronic illness and disability; for a summary of some of the main studies on this area see ABS (1994c, pp.112-113). This influences the utilisation of health services.

Lack of appropriate data on health expenditure by birthplace of the population has prevented research in this area. The only known relevant study is that of Mathews (1992) who, studying the impact of immigration on state government budgets, measured per capita expenditure on health services by country of birth. A limitation of Mathews's data in Table 6.5 is that they were was based on the 1989-90 immigration intake; that is, the health expenditure measures provided do not reflect the health status or health services utilisation of the stock of immigrants but of the inflow of immigrants in that year. According to Mathews (1992), immigrants with the characteristics of those who arrived in 1989-90 use health services more intensively than Australian-born people. The highest per capita health expenditure is for ESB people which is followed by NESB people and then Australian-born people.

6.1.5   Other Factors Influencing Social Expenditure

There are other characteristics exhibited by some birthplace groups which exert an impact on social expenditure. Some of these characteristics are discussed briefly in this subsection.

High levels of unemployment and lower access to some government services among NESB people are often attributed in part to low levels of English proficiency. According to the ABS (1994e, p.15), 30 per cent of NESB migrants aged 18 and over who arrived in Australia between 1970 and September 1993 reported low levels of English proficiency at the time of the survey.

The migration category is also related to social expenditure. For example, as mentioned above, people arriving as refugees experience high unemployment rates as well as high rates of utilisation of the welfare system. Furthermore, since some of them experienced torture and trauma prior to arrival in Australia they often require other special assistance. At least 10 per cent of all immigrants during the last 10 years have entered Australia under the Humanitarian Program; see Bureau of Immigration, Multicultural and Population Research (BIMPR) (1995, p.25).

Some studies report discriminatory behaviour in the labour market against certain birthplace groups, particularly in professional occupations; see, for example, Flatau and Hemmings (1991) and Hawthorne (1994). Jones (1992, p.109) concluded that there exists some form of 'indirect discrimination, ranging from employer preferences in hiring, training and promoting staff, to the social forces that induce women and men to make different choices about schooling, post-school training, and occupational careers'.

Johnson (1991) measured the association between educational qualifications, age, years of residence in Australia, and language of country of origin with immigrant poverty, and found that the well-being of migrants increased with post-school qualifications, period of residence in Australia, age, and where English is the language spoken in the country of origin. He concluded that NESB immigrants formed the poorest group, followed by those born in Australian, while ESB immigrants displayed the lowest level of poverty.

The time of arrival and length of residence in Australia has been mentioned above when discussing the labour force status of migrants. However, in considering the influence of the time of arrival on social expenditure an additional dimension should be included, namely, the particular stage of development of the Australian society at the time of arrival of new settlers. Within this context, two periods can be distinguished. The first period includes the immediate post-war years until the late 1960s, characterised by economic prosperity with a high demand for unskilled and low skilled workers particularly from the manufacturing industry. The second period, starting from the 1970s, is characterised by interrupted economic growth, inflation, high levels of unemployment, a declining manufacturing industry, economic restructuring, and the need for a more qualified labour force.

Many non-English-speaking born migrants, particularly from Eastern and Southern European countries, who arrived during the first period, were unskilled workers and experienced high employment and wage levels. The financial base built up during those years has made them able to cushion the effects of a more adverse labour market during recent years.

Immigrants who arrived during the last two decades have faced a more competitive labour market where English proficiency and skills are highly valued. Economic restructuring and modernisation have significantly reduced the availability of traditional low-skilled 'entry-level' jobs. Although the manufacturing industry continues to provide a significant share of jobs for NESB migrants, instability and low pay conditions characterise these occupations.

In summary, there are socio-economic differences between overseas-born people as a whole and people born in Australia, but these differences are particularly marked when comparing NESB people with those born in Australia. The characteristics exhibited by ESB people are closer to persons born in Australia than to NESB immigrants. Nothing has been said so far about whether there is a process of adjustment of the characteristics of migrants to those of the native-born people, and the social and economic changes such a process would involve. These issues are discussed in the next section.

6.2   The Adjustment Process

Studies of the effects of migration on the age structure of the population and on social expenditure have traditionally assumed that newly arrived migrants instantaneously acquire the demographic and socio-economic characteristics of the existing resident population, and that the existing resident population is homogeneous. However, previous chapters have illustrated the extent of heterogeneity among overseas-born people and between them and those born in Australia. Nevertheless, there also seems to exist an adjustment process through which the social and economic characteristics of different population groups tend to converge. That is, over time the population becomes more

Table 6.6: Unemployment Rates by Birthplace and Period of Residence:
August 1994 (percentages)

Period	ESB	NESB	Total
Before 1971	7.8	8.9	8.4
1971-75	8.7	12.5	10.6
1976-80	10.1	10.9	10.5
1981-85	9.1	16.3	13.4
1986-90	8.3	15.1	12.6
1991-94	9.9	29.5	22.3
Total	8.5	13.7	9.2

homogeneous in most of the aspects discussed above. The question arises of
the length of time required for the adjustment process to take place. If the
period required is long, the validity of projections made under the assumption
of immediate adjustment may be questioned.

Any attempt to identify adjustment processes taking place over time is
severely limited by the cross-sectional nature of the available data. For example, Beggs and Chapman (1988b), examining immigrants' wage adjustment
in Australia, found that there are biases inherent in cross-sectional work, particularly for NESB immigrants. Any process of change is obviously extremely
complex and involves many factors. No attempt is made here to provide an
explanation of the process or even to produce a simple model. Rather, the
limited available data are examined in order to see if a time scale can be
identified.

The available data suggest that an adjustment process does indeed exist though the length of time required for this process to take place varies
depending on the variables considered. Labour force status appears to be
the variable most sensitive to adjustment over time. Table 6.6, using ABS
Labour Force Survey data on microfiche (group 600, table ANI3), presents
unemployment rates by birthplace and period of residence. Although it is difficult to disentangle the effect of the calendar date of arrival from the length
of residence, there is some evidence that unemployment rates experienced by
NESB people fall substantially within a few years after arrival.

Other characteristics seem to require much more time for any adjustment towards a common path to be noticeable. For example, educational disparity among some overseas-born groups and between them and people born in Australia appears to exist over several generations. For example, according to Kee (1992, p.7), while the educational attainment of immigrant Jews was three times higher than that for the total Australian population, the proportion of second-generation Jews with a degree was double that of immigrant Jews and was more than five times higher than that of all second-generation Australians.

A more recent study by Birrell and Khoo (1995), based on 1991 Census data, documents the greater educational progress of second-generation Australians born to Southern European or Lebanese fathers, compared with second-generation Australians whose fathers were born in Australia or were ESB fathers. Although these results can not automatically be generalised to other birthplace groups or future generations, it suggests that cultural and family values associated with birthplace have an influence on social and economic outcomes and, hence, on social expenditure. Thus, it is expected that, although first generations do not exert a big impact on education expenditure, second generations use educational services at least with the same intensity as other people whose parents were born in Australia. On the other hand, given the high correlation between education and living standards, the impact of these second and later generation Australians on welfare services can be expected to be much lower than first generations.

Studies of the labour market experience of second-generation Australians are sparse. No conclusive evidence has been produced. For example, Chiswick and Miller (1985), studying immigration generations and income in Australia, estimated that Australian-born people with an Australian-born mother and a foreign-born father, all other things equal, may be able to obtain an earnings differential of 2.9 per cent compared with individuals with both parents born in Australia. Researchers have also failed to find evidence of disadvantage for immigrants arriving as children; see Evans and Kelley (1986), Miller (1986), Bradbury *et al.* (1986), Miller and Volker (1987), and Wooden *et al.* (1994). Jones (1989) and Flatau and Hemmings (1991), on the other hand, suggested that there were inter-generational labour market disadvantages associated with some NESB groups. Birrell and Khoo (1995) also reported lower earnings in almost every occupational category for some second-generation NESB groups compared with their Australian counterparts.

Appropriate data on the variability of demographic characteristics by birthplace over time are not available. However, since cultural and socio-economic factors influence demographic variables, it may be suggested that the latter, particularly fertility and mortality, probably exhibit some constancy over time.

In summarising the above discussion it can be said that any adjustment of immigrants and their descendants towards a common set of demographic and socio-economic characteristics appears to be far from instantaneous. It therefore seems desirable, in making projections, to attempt to incorporate some allowance for these differences. Population and social expenditure projections can be made assuming different degrees of adjustment of demographic and socio-economic characteristics by birthplace. This is carried out in Part IV.

Part IV

Population and Expenditure Projections

Chapter 7

Projection Techniques

This chapter presents the basic methods used to produce the population and social expenditure projections which are reported in later chapters. Section 7.1 examines some of the basic determinants of the population age structure and population growth using a social accounting framework. The analysis makes use of matrix methods, which are familiar to most economists. Section 7.2 presents the method used to obtain social expenditure projections. Hypothetical examples are then given in section 7.3

7.1 Population Projections

7.1.1 A Social Accounting Framework

Population flows can be represented by the social accounting framework shown in Table 7.1. There are N (single year) age groups. The square matrix of flows, from columns to rows, has $N - 1$ non-zero elements which are placed on the diagonal immediately below the leading diagonal. No one is assumed to survive beyond the age of N. Define the coefficients, a_{ij}, showing the proportion of people in the jth age who survive in the country to the age i, as:

$$a_{ij} = f_{ij}/p_j \qquad (7.1)$$

As stated above, only the $a_{i+1,i}$, for $i = 1, ..., N - 1$ are non-zero.

Table 7.1: Demographic Flows

	1	2	3	...	N	Births	Entrants	Total
1	0	0	0	...	0	b_1	v_1	p_1
2	f_{21}	0	0	...	0	0	v_2	p_2
3	0	f_{32}	0	...	0	0	v_3	p_3
...	...	...	...	...	...	...	...	...
N	0	0	0	...	0	0	v_N	p_N
Exits	d_1	d_2	d_3	...	d_N			
Total	p_1	p_2	p_3	...	p_N			

This framework applies to males and females separately, distinguished by subscripts m and f. Hence the matrices of coefficients for males and females are A_m and A_f respectively. Let $P_{m,t}$ and $P_{f,t}$ represent the vectors of male and female populations at time t, where the ith element is the corresponding number of age i. The N-element vectors of births and immigrants are represented by b and v respectively, with appropriate subscripts; only the first element of b is non-zero, of course. The number of people existing in one year consists of those surviving from the previous year, plus births, plus immigrants. Hence the 'forward equations' corresponding to this framework are:

$$p_{m,t+1} = A_m p_{m,t} + b_{m,t} + v_{m,t} \tag{7.2}$$

$$p_{f,t+1} = A_f p_{f,t} + b_{f,t} + v_{f,t} \tag{7.3}$$

Given population age distributions in a base year, and information about the relevant flows, equations (7.2) and (7.3) can be used to make projections. In general the matrices A_m and A_f, along with the births and inward migration flows, may be allowed to vary over time. Changes in the As can arise from changes in either mortality or outward migration.

Further specification can be added to the model by considering births. Suppose that c_i represents the proportion of females of age i who give birth per year. Many elements, for young and old ages, of the vector, c, will of course be zero, and in general the c_is may vary over time. Suppose that a proportion, δ, of all births are male, and define the N-element vector τ as the column vector having unity as the first element and zeros elsewhere. Then births in any year can be represented by:

$$b_m = \delta\tau c'p_f \tag{7.4}$$

$$b_f = (1 - \delta)\tau c'p_f \tag{7.5}$$

where c' is the transpose of the vector c, that is, the column vector written as a row. The b vectors contain only one non-zero element. Equations (7.2) to (7.5) can thus be used to make population projections, for assumed migration levels.

7.1.2 Stable Populations

If all the coefficients, represented by the elements of the A matrices and the c and v vectors, remain constant over time the population should eventually reach a stable level and age distribution. The age distribution of males and females will be such that total 'entrants' are exactly matched by total 'exits' from the country. In practice, such a stable population is unlikely ever to be experienced, given the time required for convergence from some initial non-stable distribution, so that the coefficients are bound to change before stability is reached. Yet it is sometimes useful to have an idea of the population structure towards which any given system may be thought to be approaching.

First, consider the female population. Combine (7.3) and (7.4) and set $p_{f,t+1} = p_{f,t} = p_f$. With constant migration, $v_{f,t} = v_f$ per year, so that:

$$p_f = [A_f + (1 - \delta)\tau c']p_f + v_f \tag{7.6}$$

Notice that the matrix $\tau c'$ takes the simple form:

$$\tau c' = \begin{bmatrix} c_1 & \cdot & \cdot & c_N \\ 0 & \cdot & \cdot & 0 \\ \cdot & & & \cdot \\ \cdot & & & \cdot \\ \cdot & & & \cdot \\ 0 & \cdot & \cdot & 0 \end{bmatrix} \tag{7.7}$$

Rearranging (7.6) gives:

$$[I - A_f - (1 - \delta)\tau c']p_f = v_f \tag{7.8}$$

Where I is the unit matrix. It is convenient to denote the matrix in square brackets in (7.8) as M, so that:

$$M p_f = v_f \tag{7.9}$$

This matrix takes the form:

$$M = \begin{bmatrix} 1 - (1 - \delta)\,c_1 & -(1 - \delta)\,c_2 & -(1 - \delta)\,c_3 & \text{....} \\ -a_{21} & 1 & 0 & \text{....} \\ 0 & -a_{32} & 1 & 0 \\ \text{.....} & \text{.....} & \text{.....} & \text{.....} \end{bmatrix} \tag{7.10}$$

The first few terms c_i (for $i = 1, ..., N$) will, as noted above, be zeros. However, the M matrix will in general be non-singular, so that the stable female distribution is given by:

$$p_f = M^{-1} v_f \tag{7.11}$$

The model has the property that if there are no inward female migrants, so that $v_f = 0$, then equation (7.11) represents a set of linear homogeneous equations. Given the non-singularity of M, this means that the model has only the trivial solution whereby the stable population is $p_f = 0$.

If $v_f = 0$, and denoting the matrix in square brackets in (7.6) as A_f^*, then:

$$p_{f,t+1} = A_f^* p_{f,t}$$

$$= \left(A_f^*\right)^t p_{f,1} \tag{7.12}$$

Therefore with constant birth and death rates and no migration, the total population will grow at a constant geometric rate (which may be positive or negative) while the relative age distribution will settle down to be constant whatever the form of $p_{f,1}$. The population growth will be either 'explosive' or will converge to zero, which again confirms the earlier result. The population grows steadily if the largest characteristic root of A_f^* is greater than unity, and declines steadily if the largest root is less than one. The process shown in equation (7.12) can converge to a stable value of p_f only if the matrix A_f^* has a largest characteristic root of exactly unity, which is extremely unlikely.

The stable male population is determined by substituting (7.4) into (7.2) and setting the coefficients constant, so that

$$p_m = A_m p_m + \delta\tau c' p_f + v_m \tag{7.13}$$

Substituting for p_f from (7.11) and further rearranging gives:

$$p_m = [1 - A_m]^{-1} \left[\delta\tau c' M^{-1} v_f = v_m\right] \tag{7.14}$$

A stable non-trivial solution for p_m does not therefore require any male migrants.

7.2 Social Expenditure

It has been mentioned earlier, when discussing demographic transitions, that an increase in longevity in the industrialised countries led to a demand for the introduction of some kind of government age pension and health insurance scheme. The difficulty of providing adequate personal savings for old age, combined with the strain placed both on family support and the existing sickness support schemes, which anyway covered a small minority of workers, resulted in a situation in which the aged formed the vast majority of those found to be living below a designated poverty level. At around the same time, there was much wider recognition of a role for the government in the

other areas of social insurance, such as sickness and unemployment. It is no
accident that this movement coincided with wider support for redistribution,
involving also the use of progressive income taxation.

Social insurance schemes are typically financed on a pay-as-you-go (PAYG)
basis, that is from current taxation, and pensions form by far the largest component of social expenditure. A variety of market failure arguments have been
advanced to justify the use of such social insurance. In addition, the inter-
generational transfers involved in PAYG pension schemes are often described
in terms of an implicit social contract between three generations: each generation stands to gain from such an arrangement so long as there is sufficient
productivity and population growth. The increased ageing of the population,
expected to be most prominent in the early years of the next century, has
been widely anticipated as placing great strain on this metaphorical contract.

Pensions and health are not, however, the only age-related forms of social
expenditure, and the implications of population ageing for aggregate social
expenditure are far from clear, given the many elements involved. Many
projections can perhaps be criticised for not providing sufficient sensitivity
analyses, given the wide range of assumptions and the many uncertainties
involved. A basic projection framework, which formalises the approach used
by a number of investigators, may be described as follows.

As in the previous section, the population is divided into N age groups
and the numbers in each group at time t placed in a vector p_t, where $p_t =
p_{m,t} + p_{f,t}$. The per capita social expenditures within each group are placed
in a matrix with N rows and k columns, where there are k items of social
expenditure, that is, education, medical care, pensions and so on. If this
expenditure matrix is denoted S, then the i, jth element s_{ij} measures the
per capita cost of the jth type of social expenditure in the ith age group.
Suppose that the jth type of social expenditure per capita is expected to
grow in real terms at the annual rate Ψ_j in each age group. Then define g_t
as the k-element column vector whose jth element is equal to $(1 + \Psi_j)^{t-1}$.
Aggregate social expenditure at time t, C_t, is thus equal to:

$$C_t = g_t' S' p_t \qquad (7.15)$$

where, as above, the dash indicates transposition. This could of course be complicated by allowing for expenditure per person in each category and age to differ for males and females, but such information is rarely available.

The relevant cost is not, however, the absolute value as in (7.15), but the ratio of this cost to GDP in each year. Projections of Gross Domestic Product depend on assumptions about five factors: initial productivity, defined as GDP per employed person, productivity growth, employment rates, participation rates and the population of working age.

Total employment is the product of the population, participation rates and the employment rate. Employment is calculated by multiplying the labour utilisation rate by the labour force. If U_t is the total unemployment rate in period t, the utilisation rate is $1 - U_t$. The aggregate unemployment rate is calculated by dividing the total number of unemployed persons in period t, V_t, by the total labour force in that period, L_t. The value of V_t is in turn calculated by multiplying the age distribution of unemployment rates by the age distribution of the labour force, where these differ according to both age and sex.

Let the vectors U_m and U_f be the N element age distributions of male and female unemployment rates. If the symbol ^ represents diagonalisation, whereby the vector is written as the leading diagonal of a square matrix with other elements equal to zero, the total number of people unemployed in period t is:

$$V_t = U'_{m,t}\hat{L}_{m,t}p_{m,t} + U'_{f,t}\hat{L}_{f,t}p_{f,t} \qquad (7.16)$$

The labour force in period t, L_t, is given by:

$$L_t = L'_{m,t}P_{m,t} + L'_{m,t}P_{f,t} \qquad (7.17)$$

Suppose productivity grows at the constant rate, θ. Then GDP in period t is calculated as the product of the utilisation rate, $1 - U_t = 1 - V_t/L_t$, the labour force, L_t, and productivity, whence:

$$GDP_t = \left\{ \frac{GDP_1}{(1 - U_1)L_1} \right\} (1 + \theta)^{t-1} (1 - U_t) L_t \qquad (7.18)$$

If the population age distribution, along with the sex and age specific participation and unemployment rates, are constant, then the social expenditure to GDP ratio will remain constant if all items of expenditure grow at the same rate as productivity; that is if $\theta = \Psi_j$ for $j = 1, ..., k$.

This framework illustrates that there are many assumptions required to make projections, and many potential interdependencies which are not easy to model. For example, productivity may itself depend on social expenditures and the age distribution of workers. Furthermore, participation rates and population growth are interdependent. The changing age distribution is just one component of the ratio of aggregate social expenditure to GDP, and its effects may, for example, be swamped by changes in unemployment rates.

7.3   Hypothetical Examples

The demographic and social expenditure frameworks outlined above can be illustrated by considering a hypothetical example where, for simplicity, there are just five age groups. Suppose the constant survival rates for males and females, and fertility rates, are as shown in Table 7.2. With no migration and the additional assumption that half of all births are male, the application of the population projection method gives a constant rate of population growth of 1 per cent, with age distributions as shown also in Table 7.2. Suppose there are just four categories of social expenditure, nominally defined as education, labour market related, including unemployment benefits, health and pensions. Hypothetical costs per capita are shown in Table 7.3. Suppose male participation rates are zero for ages 1 and 5, and 0.95 for the other ages, and female participation rates are 0.7, 0.7 and 0.4 for the middle three age groups. Furthermore, assume that unemployment rates are 0.05 for all age groups for males and females. If labour productivity is initially 180 units, and both productivity and all social expenditures per capita grow at a constant rate of 0.018, then total social expenditure as a rate of GDP is found to be constant at 0.2185.

Consider the alternative survival and fertility rates shown in Table 7.4. These rates represent lower mortality and fertility and imply a steady rate

Table 7.2: Population Structure 1

Age	Survival		Fertility	Age distrib		Total
	M	F		M	F	
1	0.990	0.990	0	0.2484	0.2453	0.2468
2	0.955	0.955	0.950	0.2434	0.2403	0.2418
3	0.755	0.775	0.755	0.2300	0.2272	0.2286
4	0.625	0.655	0.550	0.1719	0.1742	0.1731
5	0	0	0	0.1063	0.1130	0.1097

Table 7.3: Social Expenditure per Capita

Age	Education	Labour	Health	Pensions
1	10	0	5	0
2	8	5	4	0
3	0	5	5	0
4	0	5	12	5
5	0	0	20	25

of population growth which is negligible, and a stable relative age structure as shown in Table 7.4. It can be seen that the population in this alternative case is substantially older than in Table 7.2. With the same assumptions about productivity, unemployment and so on, as in the first case, this new population structure implies a ratio of social expenditure to GDP of 0.2394. Hence population ageing in these examples implies increased total expenditures as a proportion of GDP. These orders of magnitude reflect those of the major industrialised countries.

The higher expenditure requires correspondingly higher tax revenues and,

Table 7.4: Population Structure 2

Age	Survival		Fertility	Age		Total
	M	F		M	F	
1	0.990	0.990	0	0.2335	0.2215	0.2274
2	0.955	0.955	0.90	0.2312	0.2193	0.2251
3	0.800	0.900	0.75	0.2208	0.2094	0.2150
4	0.780	0.855	0.47	0.1767	0.1885	0.1828
5	0	0	0	0.1378	0.1612	0.1498

depending on the tax structure, increases in tax rates. This may perhaps generate pressure for some items of social expenditure to be reduced, for example by cutting state pensions and government health benefits.

It is, however, most unlikely that the changes in the population structure would occur without any other changes, for example in participation rates. Furthermore, social expenditures are also influenced by productivity and other variables. If the participation rates of women, in the middle three age groups, is increased to 0.8, 0.8, and 0.5 respectively, the social expenditure ratio would become lower, at 0.2247. If, in addition, all unemployment rates were 0.04, the ratio would be lower, at 0.2223. Higher productivity would of course reduce the ratio further, though a differential between expenditure growth of each category and productivity means that the ratio falls steadily over time. What is clear is that population ageing is just one component of the aggregate social expenditure to GDP ratio, which is sensitive to a wide range of variables. Some of the variables, such as unemployment rates, may be independent of ageing, but there are several interdependencies about which very little is known. Nevertheless, the approach described here can be used to examine the sensitivity of results to alternative assumptions, and thus to identify those elements which require further detailed attention.

Chapter 8

Population Projections

This chapter presents projections of the Australian population under different
assumptions, by applying the model described in chapter 7. The benchmark
case in section 8.1 adopts the simplifying assumption made in previous studies, that all migrants, once they arrive in the country, immediately acquire a
common set of fertility and mortality characteristics so that the composition
of the population can be ignored. Although it has been argued that these
assumptions are unrealistic, it is useful to make such benchmark projections
so that comparisons can be made. Section 8.2 presents population projections under the alternative approach that the Australian resident population
is made up of two groups which exhibit different demographic characteristics.

8.1 Benchmark Population Projections

This section presents benchmark population projections for each decade of
the period 2001-2051, and under alternative immigration assumptions. These
are based on the estimated resident population as at June 1993 (ABS, 1994a),
mortality rates as described by the *Australian Life Tables* 1985-87 (Office of
the Australian Government Actuary, 1991), and the age and sex distribution
of the inward and outward migration flows between 1988-89 and 1992-93
(DIEA, 1994). The projections assume that fertility rates remain constant
at the 1993 level. However, mortality is assumed to decline as described by
the long-term rates of annual change estimated by the ABS (1989a). Further

detailed information about the assumptions and the data used is given in the appendix to this chapter.

Four alternative levels of annual immigration, defined as permanent arrivals, are considered: 170,000 immigrants per year, which represents high immigration; 125,000 immigrants per year, which is similar to the average intake experienced during the second half of the 1980s; 80,000 immigrants per year, which is closer to the 1990's levels; and a low immigration level of 40,000 people annually. Much of the following discussion focuses on an immigration level of 80,000 people per year, with the alternative levels used for comparison purposes. These figures represent the assumed constant number of immigrants per year. The extent and age distribution of outward migration, defined as permanent departures, is assumed to remain constant at the average of the period 1988-89/1992-93, which involves approximately 27,500 people per year.

8.1.1   Age Structure

Tables 8.1 and 8.2 show population projections assuming annual immigration of 80,000 people. The figures suggest that although Australia has one of the youngest and fastest growing populations of the Western countries, it is projected to grow older rapidly during the next few decades. The proportion of people younger than 40 years of age falls from 61 per cent in 1993 to 45.7 per cent in 2051, while those aged 65 and over increases from 11.7 to 23.6 per cent during the same period.

Population ageing is projected to accelerate, particularly during the second and third decades of the next century, with the number of people aged 65 and over increasing 44 per cent between 1993 and 2011, 61 per cent during the following 20 years, and 17 per cent between 2031 and 2051. The number of people aged between 40 and 64 is projected to increase from 27 to 34 per cent of the total population between 1993 and 2011, although it falls to 31 per cent by 2041. Even more dramatic is the appearance of the 'ageing of the aged' phenomenon. While the number of people aged 65 and over is projected to increase three-fold between 1993 and 2051, those over

Table 8.1: Population Projections 2001-2021: Annual Immigration of 80,000

Age Group	1993 000s	1993 %	2001 000s	2001 %	2011 000s	2011 %	2021 000s	2021 %
1-14	3,831	22.0	3,686	19.4	3,643	17.9	3,637	16.8
15-24	2,746	16.0	2,597	13.7	2,726	13.4	2,716	12.6
25-39	4,190	24.0	4,282	22.5	4,134	20.3	4,254	19.7
40-49	2,472	14.0	2,827	14.9	2,961	14.5	2,828	13.1
50-59	1,649	9.0	2,342	12.3	2,767	13.6	2,905	13.4
60-64	713	4.0	823	4.3	1,204	5.9	1,380	6.4
65-69	686	4.0	669	3.5	963	4.7	1,191	5.5
70-74	554	3.0	611	3.2	694	3.4	1,026	4.7
75-84	646	4.0	860	4.5	904	4.4	1,215	5.6
85-99	175	1.0	293	1.5	405	2.0	459	2.1
TOTAL	17,661	100.0	18,992	100.0	20,401	100.0	21,611	100.0

74 years of age experience a four-fold increase and those aged over 84 are multiplied seven-fold. Although the ageing appears to slow down after 2031, it is projected that the number of people older than 74 years will increase by over 800,000 during the two decades to 2051.

8.1.2 Alternative Migration Assumptions

Table 8.3 shows the effect of alternative levels of immigration on the age structure of the population.

Compared with the lowest migration case of 40,000 people per year, by 2031 a level of 80,000 people reduces the proportion of those aged 65 years and over by 1.1 percentage points; it falls by 2.2 percentage points with an intake of 125,000; and by 3.1 percentage points with 170,000 migrants. However, this retarding of the ageing effect is achieved at the expense of higher population increases. By 2031 an intake of 170,000 immigrants per year increases total population by 30 per cent more than an annual intake of 40,000 immigrants.

As discussed in chapter 4, the demographic impact of migration on the country of destination also depends on the age structure of the migrant in-

Table 8.2: Population Projections 2031-2051: Annual Immigration of 80,000

| Age | 2031 | | 2041 | | 2051 | |
Group	000s	%	000s	%	000s	%
1-14	3,717	16.5	3,713	16.0	3,732	15.8
15-24	2,683	11.9	2,754	11.9	2,757	11.7
25-39	4,301	19.0	4,238	18.2	4,313	18.3
40-49	2,895	12.8	2,977	12.8	2,915	12.3
50-59	2,782	12.3	2,855	12.3	2,942	12.5
60-64	1,434	6.3	1,314	5.7	1,391	5.9
65-69	1,278	5.7	1,293	5.6	1,299	5.5
70-74	1,189	5.3	1,248	5.4	1,154	4.9
75-84	1,656	7.3	1,882	8.1	1,977	8.4
85-99	658	2.9	949	4.1	1,149	4.9
TOTAL	22,594	100.0	23,224.6	100.0	23,630	100.0

take. The younger the migrant intake, the more immigration can slow down the extent of population ageing in the destination country. Almost 60 per cent of the migrants who arrived in Australia between 1988-89 and 1992-93 were younger than 30 years. These data were used to make the projections presented in Table 8.3. To illustrate the impact of a younger cohort of immigrants, Table 8.4 shows projections of the age structure of the Australian population assuming that 80 per cent of the intake of migrants to Australia between 1988-89 and 1992-93 was made up of people younger than 30 years. This younger age structure of the migrant intake is applied to alternative immigration levels; details are given in the appendix, Table 8.18.

The younger age structure of the annual migrant intake assumed does slow down the extent of population ageing. Comparing the impact of a migrant intake of 80,000 people in Tables 8.3 and 8.4 it can be observed that by 2031 a younger immigration level of 80,000 people increases the percentage of people aged between 1 and 39 years by almost 2 percentage points, and reduces the percentage of people older than 65 by 1.1 percentage points.

In Table 8.3, that is, without assuming a younger immigrant cohort, similar changes in the age structure of the population by the year 2031 would require an increase in the migrant intake from 80,000 people to 170,000 peo-

Table 8.3: Age Structure and Immigration

Year	Immigration	Percentages aged			Total
		1-39	40-64	65+	(000s)
2001	40,000	55.3	31.7	13.0	18,652
	80,000	55.6	31.6	12.8	18,992
	125,000	56.0	31.3	12.6	19,375
	170,000	56.4	31.1	12.4	19,758
2011	40,000	50.8	34.2	15.0	19,579
	80,000	51.5	34.0	14.5	20,401
	125,000	52.2	33.8	14.1	21,325
	170,000	52.8	33.6	13.7	22,249
2021	40,000	48.3	32.9	18.8	20,260
	80,000	49.1	32.9	18.0	21,610
	125,000	49.9	32.9	17.2	23,130
	170,000	50.6	32.9	16.5	24,649
2031	40,000	46.4	31.3	22.3	20,670
	80,000	47.4	31.5	21.2	22,594
	125,000	48.3	31.6	20.1	24,758
	170,000	49.1	31.7	19.2	26,922
2041	40,000	45.0	30.6	24.4	20,703
	80,000	46.1	30.8	23.1	23,224
	125,000	47.1	30.9	22.0	26,061
	170,000	47.8	31.1	21.1	28,897
2051	40,000	44.7	30.5	24.9	20,507
	80,000	45.7	30.7	23.6	23,630
	125,000	46.6	30.8	22.5	27,143
	170,000	47.3	31.0	21.7	30,656

Table 8.4: Change in Age Distribution of Immigrants

| Year | Immigration | Percentages aged | | | Total |
		1-39	40-64	65+	(000s)
2001	40,000	55.5	31.5	13.0	18,657
	80,000	56.1	31.1	12.7	19,003
	125,000	56.8	30.7	12.5	19,392
	170,000	57.4	30.3	12.3	19,781
2011	40,000	51.4	33.7	14.9	19,614
	80,000	52.7	33.0	14.3	20,471
	125,000	53.9	32.3	13.8	21,434
	170,000	55.1	31.7	13.3	22,398
2021	40,000	49.1	32.3	18.6	20,352
	80,000	50.7	31.8	17.5	21,794
	125,000	52.3	31.3	16.5	23,417
	170,000	53.6	30.8	15.6	25,040
2031	40,000	47.4	30.8	21.7	20,848
	80,000	49.3	30.6	20.1	22,949
	125,000	51.0	30.4	18.6	25,313
	170,000	52.4	30.2	17.4	27,677
2041	40,000	46.2	30.2	23.6	20,996
	80,000	48.2	30.1	21.7	23,810
	125,000	49.9	30.0	20.1	26,976
	170,000	51.2	29.9	18.9	30,142
2051	40,000	45.9	30.1	23.9	20,943
	80,000	47.8	30.1	22.1	24,501
	125,000	49.4	30.1	20.6	28,503
	170,000	50.5	30.1	19.4	32,506

ple. Furthermore, a younger intake of migrants retards the ageing of the population without significant increases in the size of the population. For example, a younger immigration level of 80,000 people would increase the size of the population by 1.6 per cent in 2031, compared with a population 19 per cent larger which would be produced if the migrant intake were doubled from 80,000 to 170,000 people.

8.1.3 Immigration Versus Fertility

It has been shown that immigration can retard the ageing of the population and that this effect depends on the size and age structure of the migrant intake. However, immigration also increases the size of the population in the host country. As discussed in chapter 4, researchers have questioned the 'efficiency' of immigration in slowing down the extent of population ageing.

Immigration is sometimes regarded as a substitute for fertility because the ageing and size of the population resulting from low fertility rates can be compensated to a certain extent by higher levels of immigration. The question arises of whether fertility is in any sense more 'efficient' in retarding the population ageing process than immigration. Young (1988, 1990, 1994) has questioned the demographic role of immigration, arguing that immigration can only exert a very small impact on the age structure of the Australian population. This question is examined here.

The demographic assumptions used in what follows are different from those of the previous section. Declining mortality up to the year 2020 is assumed, as described by the long-term rates of annual change estimated by the ABS (1989a), along with a continuation of the 1985-86 age and sex structure of the inward and outward migration flows. Projections of the population size and age structure since 1986 are made using three alternative cases. Case A assumes a Total Fertility Rate (TFR) of 1.44 and a zero migration intake; case B keeps the level of migration at zero but increases TFR to 1.85; case C increases the intake of migrants to 150,000 per year while keeping the TFR to the original level of 1.44. The results are presented in Table 8.5.

Increasing either the fertility rates or the immigrant level produce the same effect on the proportion of people aged 65 years and over by the end of the projection period. However, higher fertility rates produce a smaller population size and an age pyramid broader at the base than high levels of immigration.

However, immigration appears to slow down the process of ageing faster than higher fertility rates. While higher fertility reduces the proportion of elderly people by 1.2 percentage points in 2011, high migration levels decrease that proportion by 2.4 percentage points. Similarly, in 2021 and 2031 high migration levels reduce the proportion of elderly people by almost 2 percentage points more than high fertility rates; see Table 8.5. Additional gains in retarding the ageing of the population are achieved when account is taken of the demographic differences between population groups. On the other hand, although immigration produces a percentage of people in the youngest age group lower than increases in fertility, it also generates a higher proportion of working-age persons, which could potentially lead to lower dependency ratios.

To illustrate the role of immigration further, Table 8.6 presents additional estimates of the proportion of people aged 65 and over. With a 50,000 intake of migrants the proportion of elderly reaches 23.5 per cent by 2046, but with 100,000 migrants or more that proportion is only reached after several centuries have elapsed. Similarly, with an intake of 150,000 migrants the proportion of elderly reaches 22.1 per cent by the year 2160, whereas that proportion is reached by 2031 when the intake is reduced to 50,000 immigrants per year.

8.2   Population Decomposition

When comparing the demographic characteristics of migrants with those of the native-born population it was found that Australia has been augmented by a migration intake with a younger age structure, higher fertility and lower mortality rates than people born in Australia. It was also found that any adjustment towards a common set of socio-economic and demographic char-

Table 8.5: Alternative Immigration and Fertility Assumptions

Year	Case	Percentages aged			Total
		1-14	15-64	65+	(000s)
2001	A	15.2	70.5	14.3	16,617
	B	18.7	67.6	13.7	17,340
	C	16.2	70.8	13.0	19,045
2011	A	14.0	68.7	17.3	16,581
	B	17.0	66.9	16.1	17,808
	C	15.3	69.8	14.9	20,818
2021	A	12.2	64.9	22.9	16,085
	B	15.9	63.6	20.5	17,989
	C	14.0	67.3	18.7	22,237
2031	A	11.0	60.8	28.2	15,112
	B	15.4	60.6	24.0	17,791
	C	13.1	64.5	22.4	23,198
2046	A	10.4	56.1	33.5	12,833
	B	15.0	59.3	25.7	16,711
	C	12.7	61.7	25.6	23,651

Table 8.6: Changing Immigration Levels and Persons Aged 65+

	Immigration 50,000			Immigration 100,000			Immigration 150,000		
Year	65+	Total	%	65+	Total	%	65+	Total	%
	(000s)	(000s)		(000s)	(000s)		(000s)	(000s)	
2001	2,411	18,172	13.3	2,448	19,004	12.9	2,484	19,836	12.5
2011	2,950	19,285	15.3	3,028	20,762	14.6	3,106	22,238	14.0
2021	3,840	20,170	19.0	4,002	22,350	17.9	4,163	24,531	17.0
2031	4,577	20,714	22.1	4,890	23,637	20.7	5,204	26,560	19.6
2046	4,880	20,753	23.5	5,465	24,795	22.0	6,050	28,836	21.0
2081	4,699	20,069	23.4	5,884	26,504	22.2	7,070	32,940	21.5
2160	4,395	18,823	23.3	6,678	29,641	22.5	8,962	40,459	22.1

acteristics is probably not instantaneous and varies according to the characteristic considered. It has also been found that although overseas-born people as a whole have different characteristics compared with people born in Australia, these differences are particularly marked when comparing NESB people with those born in Australia. Furthermore, the characteristics exhibited by ESB people are closer to people born in Australia than to NESB people. Hence, it seems useful to consider projections where the Australian resident population is regarded as being made up of just two groups. The first consists of those born in Australia and in other English-speaking countries and their descendants on the one hand; this group is referred to as AESB. The second group consists of NESB migrants and their descendants.

Assuming that demographic characteristics such as fertility, mortality and outward migration rates are constant over time, the population decomposition can then be used to make separate population projections for the AESB and NESB groups as an alternative approach to the traditional assumption that all migrants, once they arrive in the country, immediately acquire the same set of fertility and mortality characteristics as the native-born people of the country. Projections of the Australian population in the previous section were made under the traditional assumption. This section presents projections under the alternative approach of population decomposition.

Table 8.7 presents the age structure of the two components of the Australian resident population defined above, as at June 1993, which is used as the base year for projecting the population; these data are obtained from ABS (1994a) data on magnetic media. NESB people are older than AESB and are particularly concentrated in the 40-64 age group.

8.2.1   Projections of Age Structure

Tables 8.8 and 8.9 present projections of the age structure of the Australian population by the two components defined above. In making these projections, the fertility and mortality rates for persons born in Austrralia are assigned both to Australians and ESB migrants and their descendants. Fertility rates for NESB are given by the ABS (1989b, p.63). Mortality rates are

Table 8.7: Population Age Structure by Sex and Component: 1993

| Population Group | Percentages aged | | | Total |
	1-39	40-64	65+	(000s)
AESB				
Male	65	25	10	7,586
Female	62	25	13	7,687
Total	64	25	11	15,273
NESB				
Male	44	43	13	1,211
Female	45	41	14	1,176
Total	45	42	13	2,388
TOTAL				
Male	62	28	10	8,797
Female	60	27	13	8,864
Total	61	27	12	17,661

calculated by taking the ratio of the mortality rates of NESB people to total mortality, given by the ABS (1989a, pp.70-71), and applying that ratio to the rates shown in the *Australian Life Tables* 1985-1987 (Office of the Australian Government Actuary 1991). Further details of the precise numbers used are given in the appendix to this chapter.

The method used to project the population under this approach is to take each population group, AESB and NESB persons with their descendants, and its corresponding set of demographic characteristics. Then, applying the population model, projections are made for each group as if they were two separate populations. Finally, the two groups are added together for each year of the projection period to obtain projections for the total Australian population. This method assumes that each population group keeps its demographic characteristics constant during the projection period, and that they develop independently of each other so that later generations absorb the characteristics of the group into which they are born. In the case of NESB, the second and later generations throughout the projection period were obviously born in Australia, but, as explained above, for present purposes they are referred to as NESB persons.

The approach used in this section therefore represents what might be de-

Table 8.8: Population 2001-2021: Annual Immigration 80,000; 75 per cent NESB, 25 per cent ESB

Age	1993		2001		2011		2021	
	000s	%	000s	%	000s	%	000s	%
1-14	3,831	22.0	3,773	19.8	3,782	18.3	3,831	17.4
15-24	2,746	16.0	2,598	13.6	2,773	13.4	2,813	12.8
25-39	4,190	24.0	4,283	22.4	4,135	20.0	4,301	19.5
40-49	2,472	14.0	2,829	14.8	2,964	14.4	2,831	12.9
50-59	1,649	9.0	2,345	12.3	2,772	13.4	2,911	13.2
60-64	713	4.0	825	4.3	1,208	5.9	1,385	6.3
65-69	686	4.0	671	3.5	968	4.7	1,197	5.4
70-74	554	3.0	613	3.2	698	3.4	1,033	4.7
75-84	646	4.0	865	4.5	913	4.4	1,230	5.6
85-99	175	1.0	297	1.6	417	2.0	478	2.2
TOTAL	17,661	100.0	19,101	100.0	20,631	100.0	22,012	100.0

scribed as the opposite extreme from the standard assumption of population homogeneity. Both extreme cases must ultimately be regarded as unrealistic but, precisely because they are extremes, they are worthy of consideration. The vast information required to model population heterogeneity and its changing composition in a more sophisticated manner is just not available. However, it is useful to know the possible limits between which the population structure can vary.

The population projections presented in Tables 8.8 and 8.9 also assume annual immigration of 80,000 people with constant fertility rates and mortality rates falling as described by the long-term rates of annual change estimated by the ABS (1989a). It is also assumed that 75 per cent of the migrant intake correspond to NESB people and 25 per cent to ESB people. Therefore the intake of 80,000 people is divided into these proportions, and each population group is then projected.

Comparing the results shown in Tables 8.8 and 8.9 with equivalent results in Tables 8.1 and 8.2, it can be seen that the population decomposition approach produces an age pyramid which is slightly broader at the base. Thus, by 2031 the proportion of people younger than 40 years of age is

Table 8.9: Population 2031-2051: Annual Immigration 80,000; 75 per cent NESB, 25 per cent ESB

Age	2031		2041		2051	
	000s	%	000s	%	000s	%
1-14	3,999	17.2	4,049	16.8	4,159	16.7
15-24	2,807	12.1	2,950	12.2	2,988	12.0
25-39	4,444	19.1	4,409	18.3	4,578	18.4
40-49	2,898	12.5	3,076	12.8	3,017	12.1
50-59	2,788	12.0	2,861	11.9	3,042	12.3
60-64	1,439	6.2	1,319	5.5	1,396	5.6
65-69	1,285	5.5	1,299	5.4	1,306	5.3
70-74	1,197	5.2	1,256	5.2	1,161	4.7
75-84	1,676	7.2	1,904	7.9	1,998	8.0
85-99	684	2.9	985	4.1	1,190	4.8
TOTAL	23,220	100.0	24,108	100.0	24,835	100.0

projected to be one percentage point higher than in the benchmark case of Tables 8.1 and 8.2. The decomposition approach also projects a larger total population. Clearly, these results rest heavily on the fertility and mortality assumptions.

8.2.2 Alternative Immigration Assumptions

The composition of the migration intake is important because of the demographic differences between NESB and ESB migrants, and also because of the birthplace structure of the Australian population. Demographic differences between NESB and ESB immigrants affect the age structure and size of the population. Table 8.10 shows the age structure and size of the Australian population assuming annual immigration of 80,000 people using two alternative cases. Case A has an intake of 80,000 ESB people and no NESB persons, and case B has an intake of 80,000 NESB immigrants and no ESB immigrants. Comparing these results with the benchmark case presented in Tables 8.1 and 8.2, it can be observed that for case B the retarding of the ageing effect is slightly accentuated. The biggest differential between the alternative cases occurs by the end of the projection period.

Table 8.10: Age Structure Using Two Cases

Year	Case	Percentages aged				Total
		1-14	15-39	40-64	65+	(000s)
2001	A	19.8	36.0	31.4	12.8	19,090
	B	19.7	36.0	31.4	12.8	19,104
2011	A	18.3	33.5	33.6	14.6	20,580
	B	18.3	33.5	33.7	14.5	20,647
2021	A	17.3	32.4	32.4	18.0	21,903
	B	17.4	32.3	32.4	17.9	22,048
2031	A	17.1	31.3	30.7	20.9	23,033
	B	17.3	31.2	30.7	20.8	23,282
2041	A	16.6	30.5	30.3	22.7	23,814
	B	16.9	30.5	30.0	22.6	24,206
2051	A	16.4	30.4	30.3	22.9	24,406
	B	16.8	30.5	29.9	22.7	24,977

The impact of the composition of the immigrants is obviously much more pronounced in the case of the birthplace structure of the population. In case A, the number of NESB people is projected to shrink to just 6 per cent of the Australian population by 2051, whereas in case B, the number of NESB people increases to 33 per cent of the total population by the same year. Similarly, the age structure of the NESB population is significantly altered depending on the case adopted. While the proportion of the NESB population aged 75 years and over is projected to reach only 10 per cent by 2051, if migration is made up only of NESB people, that age group is projected to represent 23 per cent of the NESB people if only ESB migrants are allowed; accordingly, the size of the NESB population would shrink from 8.2 million to 1.4 million people.

In examining the benchmark case, it was found that increasing the immigrants level reduces significantly the proportion of elderly people throughout the projection period. The use of population decomposition gives similar results, accentuating the retarding of the ageing effect obtained under the standard assumption. Table 8.11 presents population projections for only two years, assuming different levels of immigration using the population decomposition approach. The four alternative immigration levels assume that

Table 8.11: Age Structure with Alternative Immigration Assumptions

Year	Immigration	Percentages aged			Total
		1-39	40-64	65+	(000s)
2001	40,000	55.4	31.6	13.0	18,757
	80,000	55.8	31.4	12.8	19,100
	125,000	56.2	31.2	12.6	19,487
	170,000	56.6	31.0	12.4	19,873
2051	40,000	46.1	29.9	24.0	21,521
	80,000	47.2	30.0	22.8	24,834
	125,000	48.1	30.1	21.8	28,562
	170,000	48.8	30.2	21.0	32,289

the intake is made up of 75 per cent NESB migrants and 25 per cent ESB migrants. Comparing these results with those presented in Table 8.3 it can be observed that for the highest three levels of immigration the decomposition approach increases the proportion of people aged between 1 and 39 years by 1.5 percentage points. In addition, in the benchmark case, the proportion of this age group in the total population reached 47.3 per cent by 2051 with an immigration level of 170,000 people, whereas a similar percentage is achieved with only 80,000 immigrants under the decomposition approach.

Data Appendix

The population projections require a substantial amount of information. The relevant details are given in this appendix. Table 8.12 gives the 1993 age structure, from ABS (1994a), for males and females. Table 8.13 gives the mortality rates by age and sex, from the Office of the Government Actuary (1991). These mortality rates are subject to annual rates of change, as shown in Table 8.14, from ABS (1989a, p.27). The age-specific birth rates are given in Table 8.14, from ABS (1994b, p.6). Settler arrivals and permanent departures are shown in Tables 8.16 and 8.17, from DIEA (1994). When examining the effects of a younger distribution of migrants, Table 8.18 is used, which assumes that the annual intake aged less than 30 years increases from 59 per cent to 80 per cent of the total.

When the population decomposition approach is used, fertility, the age distribution and mortality characteristics are those shown in Tables 8.19 to 8.23. Table 8.19 is from ABS (1989b, p.63). Tables 8.20 to 8.22 are from ABS (1994a). The data in Table 8.23 were based on Table 8.13 and ABS (1989b, pp.70-71).

Table 8.12: Estimated Resident Population: Australia 1993

A	M	F	A	M	F	A	M	F
0	135,350	128,424	34	140,659	141,538	68	62,619	69,237
1	130,247	123,805	35	139,880	140,714	69	61,432	68,453
2	133,461	126,697	36	137,698	137,807	70	56,725	65,476
3	133,053	125,976	37	138,943	138,882	71	55,239	64,993
4	130,595	124,151	38	133,475	134,675	72	52,742	65,434
5	129,765	123,741	39	131,897	133,178	73	46,985	57,287
6	129,748	123,062	40	130,940	131,407	74	38,818	50,367
7	131,538	124,616	41	130,136	129,024	75	35,941	48,353
8	131,745	126,235	42	133,916	133,750	76	34,756	47,550
9	131,510	124,950	43	129,090	126,597	77	33,188	47,041
10	132,563	125,298	44	130,163	127,024	78	31,278	45,271
11	130,270	123,802	45	130,487	126,046	79	28,201	42,719
12	131,103	123,701	46	126,394	126,394	80	24,492	38,017
13	127,066	119,857	47	117,572	113,431	81	21,238	34,633
14	127,859	120,952	48	110,533	106,752	82	18,537	32,193
15	127,988	121,350	49	105,998	101,061	83	15,954	28,340
16	129,449	122,116	50	94,700	90,113	84	13,269	24,733
17	131,500	124,847	51	95,278	90,082	85	11,059	22,122
18	135,771	129,427	52	92,805	89,018	86	9,366	19,192
19	140,435	133,760	53	87,576	82,229	87	7,666	16,449
20	145,363	138,983	54	86,383	82,365	88	6,030	13,948
21	152,933	146,943	55	82,784	79,790	89	4,718	11,149
22	153,926	149,495	56	79,773	77,755	90	3,533	9,077
23	144,792	141,145	57	77,084	75,888	91	2,987	7,720
24	138,986	136,909	58	72,203	71,628	92	2,001	6,154
25	135,633	133,161	59	71,523	70,062	93	1,541	5,068
26	133,676	132,279	60	69,508	68,553	94	921	3,383
27	134,782	134,410	61	69,771	69,238	95	622	2,545
28	136,092	136,895	62	72,947	75,580	96	428	1,903
29	143,195	142,562	63	71,711	71,368	97	274	1,429
30	144,523	144,794	64	71,371	72,645	98	197	999
31	146,745	146,415	65	70,170	73,108	99+	414	2,026
32	151,405	151,689	66	68,327	71,307			
33	146,573	145,666	67	67,944	73,662			

Table 8.13: Probability of Dying Within a Year

A	M	F	A	M	F	A	M	F
0	0.01030	0.00794	34	0.00132	0.00063	68	0.03110	0.01610
1	0.00075	0.00063	35	0.00136	0.00067	69	0.03414	0.01786
2	0.00054	0.00042	36	0.00141	0.00073	70	0.03748	0.01979
3	0.00048	0.00029	37	0.00148	0.00079	71	0.04112	0.02192
4	0.00038	0.00024	38	0.00157	0.00087	72	0.04510	0.02426
5	0.00031	0.00021	39	0.00168	0.00095	73	0.04943	0.02685
6	0.00026	0.00020	40	0.00181	0.00105	74	0.05412	0.02976
7	0.00024	0.00019	41	0.00197	0.00117	75	0.05919	0.03305
8	0.00024	0.00017	42	0.00216	0.00130	76	0.06473	0.03677
9	0.00024	0.00016	43	0.00237	0.00145	77	0.07075	0.04098
10	0.00025	0.00015	44	0.00262	0.00161	78	0.07733	0.04573
11	0.00027	0.00014	45	0.00291	0.00180	79	0.08452	0.05107
12	0.00029	0.00014	46	0.00323	0.00200	80	0.09235	0.05703
13	0.00031	0.00016	47	0.00360	0.00223	81	0.10089	0.06368
14	0.00035	0.00020	48	0.00402	0.00247	82	0.11018	0.07104
15	0.00050	0.00026	49	0.00450	0.00274	83	0.12024	0.07917
16	0.00077	0.00035	50	0.00504	0.00302	84	0.13110	0.08808
17	0.00112	0.00045	51	0.00563	0.00332	85	0.14276	0.09781
18	0.00142	0.00052	52	0.00630	0.00364	86	0.15494	0.10839
19	0.00158	0.00054	53	0.00704	0.00398	87	0.16737	0.11984
20	0.00161	0.00053	54	0.00785	0.00434	88	0.17976	0.13217
21	0.00159	0.00052	55	0.00875	0.00472	89	0.19187	0.14536
22	0.00155	0.00051	56	0.00974	0.00512	90	0.20343	0.15922
23	0.00149	0.00050	57	0.01082	0.00555	91	0.21423	0.17355
24	0.00143	0.00050	58	0.01200	0.00605	92	0.22405	0.18815
25	0.00138	0.00050	59	0.01327	0.00660	93	0.23268	0.20284
26	0.00135	0.00050	60	0.01465	0.00722	94	0.24155	0.21744
27	0.00134	0.00051	61	0.01615	0.00793	95	0.25069	0.23179
28	0.00132	0.00051	62	0.01776	0.00872	96	0.26012	0.24575
29	0.00130	0.00052	63	0.01951	0.00963	97	0.26982	0.25916
30	0.00129	0.00053	64	0.02142	0.01065	98	0.27982	0.27190
31	0.00129	0.00055	65	0.02351	0.01179	99+	0.29010	0.28387
32	0.00129	0.00057	66	0.02581	0.01308			
33	0.00130	0.00059	67	0.02833	0.01451			

Table 8.14: Long-Term Rates of Annual Change in Age-Specific Death Rates by Sex and Age Groups

Age	Males	Females
0	-0.02594	-0.02404
1-4	-0.02290	-0.01839
5-9	-0.02239	-0.01844
10-14	-0.01424	-0.01849
15-19	-0.01017	-0.00819
20-24	-0.00404	-0.00339
25-29	-0.00156	-0.00931
30-34	-0.00970	-0.00827
35-39	-0.02099	-0.01211
40-44	-0.01742	-0.01234
45-49	-0.01833	-0.00865
50-54	-0.01105	-0.00652
55-59	-0.00849	-0.00451
60-64	-0.00747	-0.00661
65-69	-0.00853	-0.00325
70-74	-0.00871	-0.00652
75-79	-0.00988	-0.00965
80-84	-0.00753	-0.01095
85-89	-0.00451	-0.01061
90-94	-0.00193	-0.00937
95-99	-0.00303	-0.00506

Table 8.15: Age-Specific Birth Rates, 1993

Age	15-19	20-24	25-29	30-34	35-39	40-44	45-49
Births per 1000	20.9	71.1	130.0	105.5	39.0	6.3	0.2

Table 8.16: Settler Arrivals by Country of Birth (Average 1988/89-1992/93)

Age	ESB		NESB	
	Males	Females	Males	Females
0-4	2,298	2,148	3,886	3,722
5-9	1,731	1,632	3,663	3,460
10-14	1,283	1,211	3,086	2,849
15-19	1,154	1,130	2,594	3,083
20-24	1,735	1,819	2,987	4,298
25-29	2,969	2,965	5,243	6,272
30-34	2,423	2,172	5,529	5,654
35-39	1,710	1,437	3,939	3,749
40-44	1,184	904	2,466	2,224
45-49	570	475	1,242	1,159
50-54	366	334	833	970
55-59	290	323	726	932
60-64	286	387	680	815
65+	664	811	879	1,018
Total	18,663	17,748	37,753	40,205

Table 8.17: Permanent Departures by Country of Birth (Average 1988/89-1992/93)

Age	ESB		NESB	
	Males	Females	Males	Females
0-4	1,446	1,372	94	97
5-9	879	831	114	119
10-14	667	665	127	134
15-19	527	594	111	131
20-24	849	1,223	168	235
25-29	1,426	1,772	312	345
30-34	1,385	1,426	374	361
35-39	1,022	946	345	317
40-44	787	679	307	241
45-49	502	446	228	173
50-54	336	281	181	127
55-59	235	191	133	115
60-64	177	194	124	132
65+	418	507	271	268
Total	10,656	11,127	2,889	2,795

Table 8.18: Alternative Age Distribution of Immigrants

Age	Males	Females	Total
0-4	8,554	7,868	16,422
5-9	7,461	6,825	14,286
10-14	6,043	5,442	11,485
15-19	5,184	5,647	10,831
20-24	6,532	8,199	14,731
25-29	11,359	12,381	23,740
30-34	3,772	3,882	7,654
35-39	2,680	2,573	5,252
40-44	1,731	1,552	3,283
45-49	860	811	1,670
50-54	569	647	1,216
55-59	482	623	1,105
60-64	458	596	1,055
65+	732	907	1,639
Total	56,416	57,953	114,369

Table 8.19: Live Births per 1,000 Females by Birthplace of Mother, 1986

Birthplace	15-19	20-24	25-29	30-34	35-39	40-44	45-49	TFR
Australia	22.1	93.0	149.0	90.9	25.8	3.9	0.2	1,925
Overseas	24.6	101.9	144.8	96.5	33.7	5.9	0.3	2,039
ESB	25.2	93.7	138.2	95.2	29.5	5.0	0.2	1,935
NESB	24.1	110.6	151.1	97.5	36.5	6.5	0.4	2,134
Total	22.2	93.3	145.8	90.9	27.8	4.4	0.2	1,923

Table 8.20: Estimated Resident Population by Single Year of Age and Sex, 1993 (People born in Australia only)

A	M	F	A	M	F	A	M	F
0	134,998	128,111	34	102,438	102,519	68	41,519	48,854
1	128,982	122,561	35	101,060	101,134	69	40,667	47,947
2	130,033	123,682	36	99,018	98,440	70	38,403	46,546
3	128,750	122,006	37	98,903	97,875	71	36,972	46,178
4	124,919	118,849	38	94,339	94,851	72	35,335	46,510
5	122,686	116,917	39	92,887	93,377	73	30,593	39,924
6	121,437	115,202	40	91,705	91,944	74	27,705	37,715
7	122,052	115,394	41	90,059	89,413	75	26,763	37,448
8	121,159	116,000	42	90,904	91,066	76	26,224	37,397
9	120,284	114,313	43	85,578	84,767	77	24,373	36,070
10	120,675	114,109	44	82,642	82,492	78	22,556	34,612
11	117,617	111,875	45	81,633	80,981	79	20,148	32,546
12	117,003	110,597	46	83,585	82,792	80	17,253	28,695
13	112,100	105,991	47	73,971	73,942	81	14,813	25,900
14	112,422	106,698	48	71,400	71,881	82	12,823	23,713
15	112,255	106,842	49	67,861	67,819	83	10,840	20,730
16	112,986	106,861	50	60,044	60,027	84	8,909	18,018
17	114,320	108,861	51	60,932	60,751	85	7,495	16,269
18	117,265	111,772	52	57,254	58,350	86	6,281	14,103
19	120,600	114,721	53	53,339	53,668	87	5,101	12,081
20	123,809	118,182	54	53,333	53,676	88	3,959	10,091
21	129,702	124,187	55	51,061	52,131	89	3,000	8,194
22	129,431	125,178	56	49,714	51,468	90	2,371	6,697
23	119,380	115,682	57	47,576	49,815	91	2,015	5,626
24	113,377	110,926	58	44,145	46,993	92	1,365	4,558
25	107,772	105,283	59	44,392	46,628	93	1,057	3,753
26	104,654	102,112	60	43,883	46,277	94	617	2,397
27	103,317	101,772	61	44,315	47,072	95	429	1,824
28	102,831	102,070	62	47,163	52,333	96	270	1,378
29	107,358	105,725	63	46,629	50,454	97	165	1,035
30	107,272	106,921	64	47,351	51,836	98	132	709
31	108,429	107,927	65	46,623	52,188	99+	180	1,145
32	111,258	111,086	66	44,881	50,391			
33	107,066	105,996	67	44,995	51,388			

Table 8.21: Estimated Resident Population by Single Year of Age and Sex, 1993 (Immigrants born in English speaking countries only)

A	M	F	A	M	F	A	M	F
0	141	111	34	16,492	16,406	68	8,856	7,784
1	424	393	35	16,409	16,146	69	8,582	8,053
2	1,173	1,034	36	16,106	16,015	70	7,695	7,980
3	1,530	1,368	37	16,435	15,979	71	7,880	8,401
4	2,046	1,867	38	15,662	15,313	72	7,976	9,112
5	2,583	2,432	39	15,910	15,344	73	7,992	9,036
6	3,010	2,903	40	15,974	15,038	74	5,365	6,315
7	3,442	3,361	41	16,251	15,100	75	4,475	5,575
8	3,785	3,701	42	17,488	16,214	76	4,277	5,239
9	3,957	3,762	43	17,792	16,031	77	4,292	5,733
10	4,235	3,884	44	19,137	17,395	78	3,942	5,432
11	4,457	4,161	45	20,363	17,866	79	3,767	5,175
12	5,141	4,828	46	20,743	18,285	80	3,408	4,933
13	5,527	5,110	47	17,829	15,867	81	3,186	4,791
14	5,813	5,351	48	16,614	14,514	82	2,987	4,857
15	5,724	5,324	49	16,268	14,419	83	2,721	4,546
16	5,814	5,535	50	14,994	13,106	84	2,432	4,162
17	6,180	5,833	51	14,516	12,541	85	2,111	3,695
18	6,432	6,249	52	13,840	12,220	86	1,892	3,207
19	6,984	6,408	53	13,390	11,509	87	1,546	2,729
20	7,604	6,942	54	13,017	11,497	88	1,289	2,515
21	8,224	7,901	55	12,457	11,094	89	1,068	1,909
22	9,142	8,655	56	11,480	10,333	90	712	1,586
23	9,332	9,381	57	10,953	9,946	91	586	1,369
24	10,095	10,148	58	10,281	9,271	92	358	1,027
25	11,287	11,317	59	9,854	8,855	93	266	855
26	12,472	12,943	60	9,267	8,493	94	183	676
27	13,659	13,853	61	9,141	8,475	95	123	511
28	14,918	15,208	62	9,172	8,672	96	105	360
29	16,215	16,273	63	9,092	7,957	97	65	266
30	16,330	16,665	64	8,769	7,870	98	35	194
31	16,873	16,695	65	8,805	7,939	99+	61	300
32	17,327	17,166	66	9,188	7,889			
33	16,860	16,544	67	9,229	8,251			

Table 8.22: Estimated Resident Population by Single Year of Age and Sex, 1993 (Immigrants born in non-English speaking countries only)

A	M	F	A	M	F	A	M	F
0	211	202	34	21,729	22,613	68	12,244	12,599
1	841	851	35	22,411	23,434	69	12,183	12,453
2	2,255	1,981	36	22,574	23,352	70	10,627	10,950
3	2,773	2,602	37	23,605	25,028	71	10,387	10,414
4	3,630	3,435	38	23,474	24,511	72	9,431	9,812
5	4,496	4,392	39	23,100	24,457	73	8,400	8,327
6	5,301	4,957	40	23,261	24,425	74	5,748	6,337
7	6,044	5,861	41	23,826	24,511	75	4,703	5,330
8	6,801	6,534	42	25,524	26,470	76	4,255	4,914
9	7,269	6,875	43	25,720	25,799	77	4,523	5,238
10	7,653	7,305	44	28,384	27,137	78	4,780	5,227
11	8,196	7,766	45	28,491	27,199	79	4,286	4,998
12	8,959	8,276	46	27,039	25,317	80	3,831	4,389
13	9,439	8,756	47	25,772	23,622	81	3,239	3,942
14	9,624	8,903	48	22,519	20,357	82	2,727	3,623
15	10,009	9,184	49	21,869	18,823	83	2,393	3,064
16	10,649	9,720	50	19,662	16,980	84	1,928	2,553
17	11,000	10,153	51	19,830	16,790	85	1,453	2,158
18	12,074	11,406	52	21,711	18,448	86	1,193	1,882
19	12,851	12,631	53	20,847	17,052	87	1,019	1,639
20	13,950	13,859	54	20,033	17,192	88	782	1,342
21	15,007	14,855	55	19,266	16,565	89	650	1,046
22	15,353	15,662	56	18,579	15,954	90	450	794
23	16,080	16,082	57	18,555	16,127	91	386	725
24	15,514	15,835	58	17,777	15,364	92	278	569
25	16,574	16,561	59	17,277	14,579	93	218	460
26	16,550	17,224	60	16,358	13,783	94	121	310
27	17,806	18,785	61	16,315	13,691	95	70	210
28	18,343	19,617	62	16,612	14,575	96	53	165
29	19,622	20,564	63	15,990	12,957	97	44	128
30	20,921	21,208	64	15,251	12,939	98	30	96
31	21,443	21,793	65	14,742	12,981	99+	173	581
32	22,820	23,437	66	14,258	13,027			
33	22,647	23,126	67	13,720	14,023			

Table 8.23: Age-Specific Mortality Rates for Non-English Speaking Born

A	M	F	A	M	F	A	M	F
0	0.00412	0.00341	34	0.00114	0.00063	68	0.02892	0.01465
1	0.00030	0.00027	35	0.00107	0.00060	69	0.03175	0.01625
2	0.00020	0.00018	36	0.00111	0.00066	70	0.03486	0.01801
3	0.00019	0.00012	37	0.00117	0.00071	71	0.03824	0.01995
4	0.00015	0.00010	38	0.00124	0.00078	72	0.04194	0.02208
5	0.00012	0.00009	39	0.00133	0.00086	73	0.04597	0.02443
6	0.00010	0.00009	40	0.00143	0.00095	74	0.05033	0.02708
7	0.00010	0.00008	41	0.00156	0.00105	75	0.05386	0.02710
8	0.00010	0.00007	42	0.00171	0.00117	76	0.05890	0.03015
9	0.00010	0.00007	43	0.00187	0.00131	77	0.06438	0.03360
10	0.00010	0.00006	44	0.00207	0.00145	78	0.07037	0.03750
11	0.00011	0.00006	45	0.00233	0.00137	79	0.07691	0.04188
12	0.00012	0.00006	46	0.00258	0.00152	80	0.08404	0.04677
13	0.00012	0.00007	47	0.00288	0.00170	81	0.09181	0.05222
14	0.00014	0.00009	48	0.00322	0.00188	82	0.10026	0.05825
15	0.00035	0.00021	49	0.00360	0.00208	83	0.10942	0.06492
16	0.00053	0.00028	50	0.00403	0.00230	84	0.11930	0.07223
17	0.00077	0.00036	51	0.00450	0.00252	85	0.12991	0.08020
18	0.00098	0.00042	52	0.00504	0.00277	86	0.14100	0.08888
19	0.00109	0.00043	53	0.00563	0.00303	87	0.15231	0.09827
20	0.00111	0.00042	54	0.00628	0.00330	88	0.16358	0.10838
21	0.00110	0.00042	55	0.00735	0.00392	89	0.17460	0.11920
22	0.00107	0.00041	56	0.00818	0.00425	90	0.18512	0.13056
23	0.00103	0.00040	57	0.00909	0.00461	91	0.19495	0.14231
24	0.00099	0.00040	58	0.01008	0.00502	92	0.20389	0.15428
25	0.00119	0.00050	59	0.01115	0.00548	93	0.21174	0.16633
26	0.00116	0.00050	60	0.01231	0.00599	94	0.21981	0.17830
27	0.00115	0.00051	61	0.01357	0.00658	95	0.22813	0.19007
28	0.00114	0.00051	62	0.01492	0.00724	96	0.23671	0.20152
29	0.00112	0.00052	63	0.01639	0.00799	97	0.24554	0.21251
30	0.00111	0.00053	64	0.01799	0.00884	98	0.25464	0.22296
31	0.00111	0.00055	65	0.02186	0.01073	99+	0.26399	0.23277
32	0.00111	0.00057	66	0.02400	0.01190			
33	0.00112	0.00059	67	0.02635	0.01320			

Chapter 9

Australian Social Expenditures

The Australian population is ageing and this will have an impact on, among other things, government budgets. Some researchers have pointed out that the budgetary impact of the demographic transition, particularly in terms of the fiscal burden for future generations, will not be as severe in Australia as in other industrialised countries. For example, Ablett (1996), following the approach developed in the US by Auerbach *et al.* (1994), estimated generational accounts for Australia which show that population ageing may not imply a disproportionately high fiscal burden for future generations of Australians. Assuming a rather conservative real per capita GDP growth rate of 0.75 per cent, an annual interest rate of 6 per cent, and no fiscal policy changes after 1990-91, Ablett's calculations show a net benefit for future generations which amounts in present value terms to $62.7 thousand. Alternative calculations, using reasonable growth and interest rate assumptions, render a similar qualitative conclusion that future generations of Australians may fare better than current generations.

However, population ageing will change collective needs and the composition of public expenditure, particularly those of a social nature. Therefore, it is important to examine the institutional arrangements and structure of social expenditures in the Australian context. The items of social expenditure considered here are government outlays on social and welfare programs which vary with age. These outlays can be broadly classified in two categories. One is the provision of care and services, such as medical care, housing and education. The other is the provision of income support, which includes pensions and other benefits and allowances. The latter is basically a Commonwealth Government responsibility, whereas the provision of care and services is funded and delivered by the three tiers of government.

Section 9.1 focuses on the income support provided through the Social Security and Welfare function of the Commonwealth budget, particular attention is paid to the characteristics of the Age Pension and the superannuation arrangements brought about by the introduction of the Superannuation Guarantee Charge (SGC). The provision of care and services, specifically in the areas of health and education, is discussed in section 9.2.

9.1   Income Support

Income support is provided directly in the form of benefits paid to recipients, and in a more indirect fashion through tax rebates and other concessionary tax measures for people who meet certain criteria. This section deals with the direct forms of income support, which are mostly provided through the Social Security and Welfare function of the Commonwealth budget. Over one-third of the total Commonwealth government budget outlays during the last five years have been allocated to the achievement of this function. Another relatively small proportion of income support is provided through budget outlays which seek to achieve Education and Housing functions, such as income support for students and rent assistance for low income earners and pensioners.

The administration of these direct forms of income support is principally carried out by the Department of Social Security (DSS) and the Department of Veterans' Affairs (DVA). Given that the Age Pension represents the largest and fastest growing single item of the Social Security and Welfare function, comprising 27 per cent of total Social Security and Welfare outlays in 1995-96, the following discussion focuses on the Australian retirement income system.

9.1.1 The Retirement Income System

Australia's retirement income system is currently made up of three components, namely, the means-tested non-contributory age pension, a compulsory superannuation system, and voluntary superannuation and other private savings for retirement. According to the DSS (1995b) there were some 1.6 million beneficiaries of the publicly funded age pension in 1994-95, which absorbed $12 billion or over one-third of the total DSS program outlays. To this, it has to be added that the Department of Veterans' Affairs makes pension payments to a further 58,000 beneficiaries at a cost of $44.5 million in 1994-95. There are also tax concessions for superannuation, which are estimated to account for an additional $5.5 billion a year. The government has also made a commitment to match employees' superannuation contributions up to a maximum of 3 per cent and subject to means testing; it is estimated that the cost of these contributions would be $4.5 billion in 2001-02; see DSS (1995b, p.98). However, the future of this government commitment is uncertain.

9.1.2 The Age Pension

The age pension was introduced in Australia in 1909 with the objective of alleviating poverty among the aged. Pension benefits are flat-rate, non-contributory and not linked to workforce participation. Benefits are funded out of general revenue and are taxable but with a tax allowance almost equal to the pension benefit, so that pensioners receiving only the government pension do not pay income tax. Pension benefits are means tested.

The pension is indexed twice a year according to rises in the Consumer Price Index, and it is maintained at a level equal to at least 25 per cent of male total average weekly earnings. According to the DSS (1995b, p.107), 'At June 1995, single pensions were 25 per cent of male total average weekly earnings (MTAWE) and 32.7 per cent of disposable MTAWE (that is, after deduction of tax and Medicare levy from MTAWE). For those who are eligible for Rent Assistance, when that payment is added, pension rates increased even further over time in comparison with AWE'. At December 1994, there were 931,455 DSS recipients of Rent Assistance and 39 per cent of them were pensioners. Besides, pensioners can also be eligible for pharmaceutical allowances, telephone allowances, and other Commonwealth and State and Territory governments concessions covering energy and water charges, motor vehicle registration and public transport. The aggregate value of these fringe benefits is considerable.

However, there are concerns about the adequacy of the age pension to meet the needs of the aged, particularly after housing costs are taken into account. Thus, according to EPAC (1994, p.50):

> Consideration of the relative poverty level for over 65 year olds whose principal source of income is a government pension shows that, after housing costs are taken into account, some 7%, or 66,000 people, were living below the poverty line in 1989-90 ... At that time there were less than 5% of over 65 year olds whose principal source of income was a government pension who rented privately. However, this group is at particular risk of poverty, with nearly half of the private renters estimated as being below the poverty line.

Another issue which has received much attention recently is the means testing of the age pension. Except for a brief period during the 1970s, under the Whitlam Government, since its introduction the receipt of the age pension has been subject to means tests whose strength has changed over time. Pension payments are reduced by 50 cents in the dollar for each additional dollar of income over certain limit. Knox (1995) highlighted the main advantages and disadvantages of a means-tested age pension. He argued that the main advantage of means testing is that it allows a better targeting of benefits to those in the greatest need, which may lead to higher benefits and lower overall government costs, while at the same time encouraging an attitude of self provision.

The major disadvantage of a means-tested age pension, on the other hand, is that it discourages work effort and the accumulation of wealth beyond the exempt levels. Because most workers reach retirement age, it is argued that the perverse incentives of means tests on the age pension have higher negative economic effects than occur with other welfare payments. According to the ABS (1990) approximately three quarters of Australians aged over 65 had a government pension or benefit as their main source of income in 1990. EPAC estimates that by 2051 a similar proportion of elderly people may still be eligible for at least a part government pension; see EPAC (1994, p.49). However, there are currently no signs of a movement towards a universal age pension.

9.1.3 The Superannuation Guarantee Charge

The biggest change in Australian retirement incomes policy in recent years has been the introduction of the Superannuation Guarantee Charge (SGC), which makes savings for retirement compulsory. Commencing with 3 and 4 per cent of award wages for small and large employers respectively, employers were required after 1 July 1992 to contribute minimum pension benefits for all employees. This initial mandated contribution is planned to rise by one percentage point each two years until it reaches 9 per cent in 2002.

The Federal Government, in its 1995-96 budget announced plans to introduce compulsory employee contributions, starting in 1997-98 with 1 per cent of award wages, increasing to 2 per cent the following year, and 3 per cent the next year. Employee contributions of people earning less than double average weekly earnings were proposed to be matched by government contributions of up to $1,000 per year, which is about 3 per cent of average award wages. This means by 2002 Australians would be allocating 15 per cent of wages into superannuation. This is the level of contribution estimated to be able to generate an adequate retirement income for a male employee with 40 years of full-time employment. This level of contribution may not be sufficient to provide an adequate retirement income in the case of individuals with an interrupted working history, or as a result of erratic investment earnings, or due to withdrawing the benefits before the investment plan reaches full maturity. The Australian retirement income system also provides tax incentives for individuals willing to make additional voluntary contributions on top of the mandatory 3 per cent level. Thus, the current arrangements of the Australian retirement income system reflects the three-pillar system suggested by the World Bank in 1994, namely, a government tax-funded age pension, a mandatory fully funded and privately managed pension system, and voluntary superannuation contributions with some taxation support.

However, Knox (1995, 1996) argued that the current arrangements of the Australian retirement income system, particularly its mandated superannuation contribution of 15 per cent of earnings, puts too much reliance on only one of the three pillars, which is at odds with the diversification approach suggested by the World Bank. Knox also points out that the lack of integration between the three components of the system and the inequities derived from the taxation arrangements (which consist basically of a 15 per cent rate on contributions and investment income) make the current retirement income system inefficient. The major inefficiencies of the system are reflected in that it discourages work efforts and savings, and weakens long-term confidence in the system and equity between generations. Knox makes a case for an universal public pension, with the extra costs of such a system offset by additional taxation on superannuation benefits of high income individuals who will receive the greatest additional benefit from a universal pension. Knox also argues that using such a source of funding for the extra costs of a universal pension system, could even lead to improve the overall redistributive impact of the tax and welfare system.

Projections of the size of the Australian superannuation funds between 1995 and 2030 presented by Knox (1996, pp.200-201), shows that, including only the minimum employer contributions, these assets will raise from the current level of about 42 per cent of GDP to about 68 per cent of GDP. Superannuation assets will raise to about 74 per cent of GDP with the addition of the employee contributions, and to about 86 per cent of GDP with the addition of the employee and government contributions. This growth is expected to occur predominantly between now and 2010.

Nevertheless, even though superannuation funds will boost Australian savings substantially, government pension outlays will be little affected by the SGC during the next few decades. Projections presented by the Retirement Income Modelling Task Force suggest that by the middle of the next century

SGC provisions will lead to a reduction of government pension outlays of about 0.5 per cent of GDP; see FitzGerald (1993).

The introduction of the Superannuation Guarantee Charge represents a step towards increasing private provision. But the Australian retirement income system needs further improvement. For example, Rosenman and Warburton (1996) argue that the retirement income system is structured under the assumption that older people are not, and should not be, working. Continued employment of older workers is discouraged with such policies as high reduction rates on the Age Pension payments and high taxation on incomes above certain limits, the access to superannuation funds after age 55, the reduction of job search and reporting requirements for people over age 55 receiving unemployment benefits. All these arrangements lead to create expectations about the 'appropriate' age for retirement.

These retirement arrangements, combined with labour market restructuring and employers and community attitudes towards older workers, lead to many older workers being almost forced out of the labour market. By August 1993, males over 55 years of age accounted for 10 per cent of the male labour force and for 17 per cent of all long-term unemployed males; see Rosenman and Warburton (1996, p.57). In many cases older workers are prime targets for retrenchment. This situation is more frequently experienced by non-English-speaking background immigrants, particularly women as documented by Winocur *et al.* (1994), Rosenman and Warburton (1996). As an alternative to reduced job opportunities in the traditional salary-earner section of the labour market, many older workers are turning towards self-employment, contract employment and consulting work: in 1993, almost one quarter of workers aged 55 and over were self-employed, which compares with 9 per cent of those aged 15-54; see Rosenman and Warburton (1996, p.59). In other cases, superannuation funds, through early retirement, are in fact being used to finance unemployment in old age.

9.2   Provision of Care and Services

The provision of care and services is the other side of the social and welfare programmes coin. Both sides, income support and care, are important to develop a coherent government approach to the implications of population ageing. The provision of adequate housing and community amenities, education and health services, is as important as income support during the transition towards an older population. The 1995-96 Commonwealth budget allocations to those three functions reached $30.5 billion or 24 per cent of that year's budget, with health expenditures absorbing more than half, $18.6 billion; see Commonwealth of Australia (1996). To this it has to be added State and Territory as well as Local Government contributions. This section focuses on the health and education systems.

9.2.1   The Health System

The Australian health care system involves the three tiers of government as well as private providers particularly in the medical and dental care areas. The Commonwealth administers the universal medical schemes for private medical services, known as Medicare, and for pharmaceuticals; the State and Territory governments have the major responsibility for public health and public provision of health services, particularly the hospital systems; local governments are mainly involved with environmental control and personal preventive and home care services; see AIHW (1996, p.117).

The combined health expenditure of the three tiers of government and the private sector in Australia was $36.7 billion in 1993-94 or 8.6 per cent of that year's GDP, that is an average of $2,066 per person. Of this total, 45 per cent was contributed by the Commonwealth, 22 per cent by State and Local governments, and 33 per cent by the private sector. From 1975-76 to 1993-94, real per person health expenditure increased at an annual average rate of 2.1 per cent, with one-quarter of this increase attributed to the ageing of the population; see AIHW (1996, p.122). The largest allocations of the $34.2 billion of recurrent health expenditure in 1993-94, were for acute hospitals, 35.7 per cent, medical services, 20.1 per cent, pharmaceuticals, 11.9 per cent, and nursing home care, 7.7 per cent; see AIHW (1996, pp.127-128).

9.2.2 Health Expenditure Growth

Health expenditure is closely associated with the age structure of the population. Health expenditure per person aged over 75 is estimated to be more than 4 times greater than the average per person health expenditure, and 13 times larger than health expenditure per person aged under 16; see EPAC (1994) and Creedy and Taylor (1993). Furthermore, EPAC (1994, p.37) reported that almost half of the expenditure for those over 75 years was for the 13 per cent of that age group who were expected to die in the the the next two years. The remaining 87 per cent only spend 2.7 times the average for the population as a whole, whereas those who are within two years of death are spending 16 times the average. However, it is estimated that ageing population structures could have only added 0.3 per cent to the annual growth in health spending during the 1990s compared with real health spending growth of 4 per cent per annum in Australia; see OECD (1995b, p.95).

Demand and supply factors, other than population ageing, are more important in explaining health expenditure growth. These factors include, rising incomes, increased access and insurance cover, improvements in technology and increases in the supply of medical personnel and in physical facilities. The former Commonwealth Department of Health and Community Services estimated that every extra doctor generates on average an annual Medicare outlay of $200,000. The Australian government has been implementing controls to reduce the impact of these factors on health expenditure growth. These measures include the exercise of Medicare's monopsony power to keep medical-specific inflation low, controlling the pace of introduction of new technology and trying to control the high growth in service volumes in the fee-for-service sectors.

Among these 'top-down' expenditure controls, the major source of restrain on health expenditure growth in Australia during the 1980s was the capped budgets for public hospitals. Steps were also taken to slow the growth of nursing homes. Bed numbers were frozen at the 1983 level and access was made subject to an assessment of need. There has also been a shift in the balance between nursing home and hostel places; the frail elderly who are still mobile have been redirected towards the less costly alternatives of supported accommodation, that is hostels, or, if they are not so frail, their own homes, but with domiciliary support services; see OECD (1995b, pp.95-104).

Those changes in the provision of care to the elderly are in line with cost differentials between alternative residential arrangements, with nursing home care being the dearest option and care at home the most cost effective alternative. Patients in nursing homes can receive Commonwealth subsidies of about $80 per day, and hospital patients receive similar State Government or health fund payments. Residents of government funded hostels receive a subsidy of $33 per day from the Commonwealth, while those who have been geriatrically assessed as being eligible for institutional care but who remain at home generate an entitlement of $3.70 a day paid by the Commonwealth to their carer. Individuals resident at home or in private accommodation may also be entitled to HACC services; see EPAC (1994, p.79).

The above mentioned measures emphasise constraints on growth in total expenditures rather than on altering microeconomic incentives to improve efficiency with which resources are utilised. Some microeconomic reforms have also been implemented, though not in all States and not on a broad enough basis. These microeconomic reforms include reforms to improve the value of private health insurance, limiting fee-for-service payment arrangements, policing overservicing by doctors, introduction of co-payments and casemix funding for public hospitals; see OECD (1995b, pp.104-107).

9.2.3   The Education System

The Australian education system is a major responsibility of State and Territory governments, which administer and fund primary and secondary schools as well as technical and further education (TAFE). Although higher education institutions operate under State legislation, their funding is a Commonwealth government's responsibility. The Commonwealth is also responsible for the provision of education services to Aboriginal and Torres Strait Islander people and to migrants, and for the provision of financial assistance to students. In 1993-94, Australia's total expenditure on education was $24.9 billion or 5.8 per cent of GDP. Of this, government expenditure represented 89 per cent, with the remaining attributed to the private sector; see ABS (1996b, pp.273-279).

School attendance is compulsory for people aged 6 to 15, but high proportions of students continue at school beyond that age, with 75 per cent remaining until Year 12 in 1994. Almost half of those aged 15 to 24 were enrolled at an educational institution in September 1994. However, participation in education decreases with age. For example, among those enrolled in TAFE vocational courses in 1992, almost one quarter of them were aged 17 to 19, whereas the participation rate of 25 to 29 year-olds was 9.4 per cent, and that of 30 to 64 year-olds was 5.4 per cent. Similarly, 60 per cent of all students enrolled at higher education institutions in 1994 were younger than 25 years; see DEET (1995, pp.59-66).

The education sector experienced a rapid expansion since the mid 1980s, which translated into higher participation and retention rates and high educational attainment, with 39 per cent of Australians aged 15 to 64 having completed a recognised post-school qualification in May 1994. Although this growth is expected to moderate during the next decade, Australia is expected to have a more qualified population by 2005. For example, the proportion of people completing secondary school or holding a tertiary qualification is expected to rise from 57.2 per cent in 1994 to 67.9 per cent in 2005. The proportion of people holding a vocational education and training qualification is expected to rise from 17.9 per cent to 19.4 per cent, and the proportion of people holding a higher education qualification is likely to rise from 18.7 per cent to 23 per cent over the same period; see DEET (1995, p.81).

Chapter 10

Social Expenditure Projections

The population projections show an increase in the proportion of older people during the next few decades. Immigration can retard the ageing process to a certain extent depending on the level and demographic characteristics associated with the birthplace composition of immigrants. This demographic change in age structure and composition of the population has social and economic implications which are reflected in, among other things, changes in government social expenditure.

Projections of social expenditure associated with those changes can be made. As an indication of the potential financial requirements, it is useful to express government social expenditure as a ratio of GDP. As with the population projections, the ratio of social expenditure to GDP can be projected under the traditional assumptions which ignore the composition of the population, and under the alternative approach of population decomposition.

The data used in projecting social expenditure are described in section 10.1. Social expenditure projections under the traditional or benchmark case is the subject of section 10.2. The treatment of population decomposition and social expenditure is presented in section 10.3.

10.1 The Data

The details of the method used to project the ratio of social expenditure to GDP were described in chapter 7. The approach involves the production of projections of GDP over the relevant period, along with the levels of social expenditure on a variety of expenditure categories. The GDP projections depend on the labour force participation and unemployment rates of males and females in each age group, along with the rate of productivity growth. Using per capita social expenditures in each age group, for different categories, and making assumptions about their growth over the period, aggregate social expenditure can be calculated.

The projections consequently require data relating to the age distribution of the population, the social expenditure per head in the base period for each category, assumptions about growth per spending category, age and sex-specific participation and unemployment rates, the GDP figure for the base period and assumptions regarding future productivity growth. The age and sex distribution of the population for the projection period are given by the population projections discussed in chapter 8.

10.1.1   Social Expenditure Data

Data on social expenditure were obtained from Commonwealth and State spending figures for 1988 presented in Commonwealth Department of Community Services and Health (CDC), Policy Development Division (1990, pp.18-25, 28). The spending breakdown was much more detailed for Commonwealth than for State outlays. The information on Commonwealth expenditure included age pensions, unemployment benefits, health, social welfare, employment and education. State figures, on the other hand, covered only the broad groupings of welfare, health and education. Dividing the sum of total State and Commonwealth expenditure in each category and age group by the total population age distribution at June 1988 (ABS, 1989c) gives per capita spending. These data and calculations are presented in Creedy and Taylor (1993a, p.48, pp.55-56) and are reproduced in Tables 10.1 and 10.2. The values are in dollars at 1988 prices.

The data on employment costs in Table 10.2 may underestimate total social spending in this category because data for State spending on employment in CDC (1990) were not included as a separate category. State employment

Table 10.1: Social Expenditure Costs per Year per Head

Age	Age Pension	Other Age Assistance	Unemployment Benefits	Other Social Security
0-15	0	3.64	0	882.98
16-24	0.30	1.84	384.46	345.89
25-39	1.12	1.67	300.21	422.62
40-49	6.19	2.78	211.03	502.82
50-59	57.19	5.86	215.20	1087.91
60-64	1138.77	12.15	184.49	1729.03
65-59	2430.04	30.82	0	2041.46
70-74	3368.12	59.93	0	1625.66
75+	4168.33	262.61	0	1134.58

Table 10.2: Social Expenditure Costs per Year per Head

Age	Health	Education	Employment	Total
0-15	443.15	913.00	1.89	2244.66
16-24	443.36	1528.55	165.32	2869.72
25-39	602.43	303.21	59.25	1690.51
40-49	565.05	140.69	37.75	1466.31
50-59	941.80	57.56	24.66	2390.18
60-64	1579.01	24.27	13.39	4681.11
65-69	2185.35	15.57	0	6703.24
70-74	3254.59	16.23	0	8324.53
75+	6110.80	12.38	0	11688.70

spending not included in State welfare payments is therefore excluded from this study.

The expenditure category 'other social security' includes Commonwealth asssistance to veterans, the handicapped, families, sole parents and widowed people, and other welfare payments such as outlays for funerals and temporary accommodation. State welfare payments are also included.

Tables 10.1 and 10.2 show the main items of government social expenditure that vary with age. Unemployment benefits, education, and expenditure on employment programmes are concentrated on people under 60 years of age, while the rest of government social expenditure increases substantially when people reach 60 years and over. In total, social expenditure per head on people aged 75 and over is 5.2 times higher than public outlays on people under 16 years of age. Unfortunately the available data do not give these costs separately for males and females.

The change in the relative importance of different types of public spending may cause a change in the mix of Commonwealth and State outlays. For example, if education spending falls and aged assistance and health outlays rise as a result of the ageing population, Commonwealth social outlays will increase in importance relative to State social outlays, assuming no change in current policies.

10.1.2   Participation and Unemployment Rates

Age and sex-specific participation and unemployment rates of the labour force are shown in Table 10.3, from Creedy and Taylor (1993a, p.49). These rates are assumed to be constant throughout the projection period, although it would be a straightforward matter to allow them to vary in a specified way. Creedy and Taylor (1993a, 1993b) conducted sensitivity analyses where explicit allowance was made for changes in unemployment rates and their effect on the growth rate of expenditure on unemployment benefits.

Table 10.3: Unemployment and Participation Rates (percentages)

	Unemployment Rate		Participation Rate	
Age	Males	Females	Males	Females
0-14	0.0	0.0	0.0	0.0
15-24	12.8	13.4	73.5	65.9
25-39	5.3	6.9	94.6	64.5
40-49	4.2	4.8	93.3	66.3
50-59	4.9	4.5	80.7	41.8
60-64	8.7	1.0	48.7	13.3
65-69	0.4	0.0	13.4	4.6
70-74	0.6	0.0	9.3	2.2
75+	0.0	0.0	4.4	0.9

10.2 Benchmark Expenditure Projections

The benchmark projections focus on the effects of the changing population age structure on social expenditure, holding all other factors influencing public expenditure constant. The increase in the proportion of older people in the population, holding participation and unemployment rates and real outlay levels constant and assuming no changes in government social policy, causes the structure of total public social expenditure to change. The number of recipients for each different government social expenditure programme will rise or fall depending on whether the programme focuses on the old or the young. For example, as the number of people over the age of 65 rises, the number of persons claiming the age pension will increase, causing total public pension payments to increase. However, a concurrent fall in the number of people younger than 25 years will reduce the number of recipients for education spending.

Social expenditure projections in this section are based on the benchmark population estimates presented in chapter 8. Expenditure projections are made for the period 2001-2051, taking 1988 as the base year. The GDP figure for 1987-88 is $241,889 million, and productivity and per capita costs in each social expenditure category are assumed to grow at 2 per cent per annum. Table 10.4 presents social expenditure projections for a population

Table 10.4: Social Expenditure Projections by Category ($ Millions)

Category	1988	2001	2011	2021	2031	2041	2051
Age P	6,963	12,401	18,426	29,006	43,521	59,497	76,087
Other A	279	539	756	1,163	1,841	2,641	3,476
U. Bens	3,150	4,575	5,884	7,300	8,897	10,901	13,440
Other S	12,683	19,434	26,911	36,360	47,234	59,351	73,883
Health	16,174	27,124	37,615	53,950	76,748	102,982	131,577
Ed	9,188	11,929	14,815	18,099	22,190	27,352	33,497
Empl	821	1,120	1,417	1,739	2,115	2,610	3,202
Total	49,258	77,124	105,823	147,618	202,547	265,335	335,162

age structure estimated assuming annual immigration of 80,000 people, which is the same population age structure as that presented in Tables 8.1 and 8.2. The categories are the same as those used in Tables 10.1 and 10.2.

Most social expenditures are concentrated in only three categories: these are health, other social security, and age pension. These categories are highly sensitive to population ageing, particularly age pension and health expenditures. In 1988, 73 per cent of total social expenditure was concentrated in those three categories. By 2031 it is projected that 83 per cent of social expenditure will be made up of health, other social security, and age pension expenditures. This means an absolute increase in expenditure from 36 billion to 168 billion dollars (in constant 1988 prices) during that period.

Expenditures on age pensions are projected to experience the fastest growth, with an eleven-fold real increase between 1988 and 2051. Most of that increase occurs during the first four decades of the projection period, reflecting the pattern of population ageing. Health expenditures are projected to increase eight-fold from 16 billion in 1988 to 132 billion dollars in 2051. As with age pensions, most of that rise is projected to occur during the first decades of the next century.

The trends described above are reflected in the social expenditure to GDP ratios. As the population ages, education spending as a proportion of GDP decreases, while expenditure on the age pension, other age assistance and health increase as a proportion of GDP. The aggregate social expenditure

Table 10.5: Ratio of Social Expenditure to GDP by Category

Category	1988	2001	2011	2021	2031	2041	2051
Age Pension	0.0288	0.0340	0.0394	0.0500	0.0612	0.0680	0.0707
Other Age	0.0012	0.0015	0.0016	0.0020	0.0026	0.0030	0.0032
Unem. Ben	0.0130	0.0125	0.0126	0.0126	0.0125	0.0125	0.0125
Other SS	0.0524	0.0533	0.0575	0.0626	0.0664	0.0678	0.0686
Health	0.0669	0.0744	0.0804	0.0929	0.1079	0.1176	0.1222
Education	0.0380	0.0327	0.0317	0.0312	0.0312	0.0312	0.0311
Employment	0.0034	0.0031	0.0030	0.0030	0.0030	0.0030	0.0030
Aggregate	0.2036	0.2115	0.2261	0.2542	0.2847	0.3031	0.3113

ratio is projected to increase because of the combined effect of population ageing and the fact that expenditure per capita on old people is projected to be much higher than that on younger age groups. Table 10.5 shows the ratio of social expenditure to GDP corresponding to the dollar amounts presented in Table 10.4. At an aggregate level, the social expenditure to GDP ratio is projected to increase by about 50 per cent, from approximately 0.2 to 0.3, during the projection period, and total social expenditure rises from 49 billion in 1988 to 335 billion dollars in 2051.

This projected increase in the social expenditure ratio, from about a fifth to a third of GDP by the middle of the next century, is similar to earlier results obtained by Creedy and Taylor (1993a) and EPAC (1994).

10.2.1 Alternative Immigration Assumptions

In examining the impact that alternative levels of immigration can have on the social expenditure ratio, Table 10.6 presents the aggregate social expenditure to GDP ratio under alternative immigration assumptions. It can be seen that higher levels of immigration might be expected to retard the growth of the social expenditure to GDP ratio. For example, by 2031, an immigration level of 40,000 is projected to produce a social expenditure to GDP ratio of 0.2956, whereas with an annual intake of 170,000 people that ratio is projected to be 0.2665. Under a migration level of 40,000 immigrants, the ratio of social expenditure to GDP is projected to increase by about 6.6

Table 10.6: Aggregate Social Expenditure to GDP Ratios

Immigration	1988	2001	2011	2021	2031	2041	2051
40,000	0.2036	0.2128	0.2298	0.2615	0.2956	0.3158	0.3245
80,000	0.2036	0.2115	0.2261	0.2542	0.2847	0.3031	0.3113
125,000	0.2036	0.2101	0.2224	0.2472	0.2747	0.2921	0.3003
170,000	0.2036	0.2087	0.2190	0.2411	0.2665	0.2834	0.2921

percentage points between 2011 and 2031, but with 170,000 immigrants the increase is projected to be about 4.8 percentage points over the same period. Thus, although higher immigration levels increase the size of the population, the impact of immigration on the age structure of the population, holding all other factors influencing public expenditure constant, is to restrain the growth of the ratio of social expenditure to GDP during the projection period.

As shown in chapter 8, the retarding of the ageing effect is greater the younger the migrant intake. So it would also be expected that the slowing down of the rate of growth of the social expenditure to GDP ratio would be stronger with a younger migrant intake. This is illustrated in Table 10.7 which presents projections of the aggregate social expenditure to GDP ratios corresponding to the age structure of the Australian population which would result from a younger migrant intake such as that assumed in calculating the values shown in Table 8.4 in chapter 8, where it was assumed that the participation of immigrants younger than 30 years increased from 59 per cent to 80 per cent of the total immigrant intake.

Comparing the values in Tables 10.6 and 10.7 it is observed that a younger migrant intake, through slowing down the extent of population ageing, retards the growth of the ratio of social expenditure to GDP. For example, by 2031 a younger migrant intake of 80,000 people would reduce the social expenditure to GDP ratio by 0.0079; the fall would be 0.0139 by 2051. As expected, the fall in the ratio increases with the size of the intake of immigrants. By 2031, a younger migrant intake of 40,000 people would reduce the ratio by 0.0046. By the same year, the fall would be 0.0128 with a younger

Table 10.7: Social Expenditure to GDP Ratios with Younger Migrants

Immigration	1988	2001	2011	2021	2031	2041	2051
40,000	0.2036	0.2131	0.2297	0.2599	0.2910	0.3085	0.3158
80,000	0.2036	0.2120	0.2260	0.2513	0.2768	0.2910	0.2974
125,000	0.2036	0.2109	0.2222	0.2430	0.2640	0.2762	0.2827
170,000	0.2036	0.2098	0.2188	0.2360	0.2537	0.2648	0.2719

immigrant intake of 170,000 people.

Given the age structure of the immigrant intake to Australia between 1988-89 and 1992-93, the social expenditure to GDP ratio is projected to be 0.2921 by the year 2051 if 170,000 immigrants settle in Australia each year of the projection period. A similar social expenditure to GDP ratio could be achieved by the year 2051 with only half that intake of immigrants, but with an increase in the participation of immigrants younger than 30 years from 59 per cent to 80 per cent of the total annual intake.

10.3   Population Decomposition

The previous section has shown that, as the Australian population continues to age, the ratio of government social expenditure to GDP is projected to increase. The precise extent of this increase depends on a number of variables, among them the immigration level and age structure. Altering the age structure of the population is one way in which immigration may affect social expenditure, and section 10.2 showed how the impact of younger intakes of immigrants and higher immigration levels on the age composition of the population retards the growth of the social expenditure to GDP ratio. However, in considering the full impact of immigration, it seems desirable to take account of the social and economic characteristics of immigrants, which, as discussed in previous chapters, vary according to their birthplace composition. Demographic as well as socio-economic characteristics of migrants born in countries where English is not the main language (NESB migrants), and to some extent their descendants, are different from those born in the main

English-speaking countries (ESB migrants).

The impact of these differences on social expenditure projections is examined in this section. Firstly, the impact of the composition of the population on the rate of growth of social expenditure is discussed. Social expenditure projections are then obtained and compared with the results from the benchmark case in section 10.2. The population estimates used in this section are those generated under the population decomposition approach.

10.3.1   Birthplace Composition and Social Expenditure Growth

In projecting social expenditure it has been assumed that expenditure per person in each category of social expenditure grows at the same rate as productivity, that is, at an annual rate of growth of 2 per cent. Other factors that can affect the rate of growth of social expenditure, such as unemployment and participation rates, have been assumed to be constant. However, it has been seen that, for example, the rates at which people received Social Security payments were higher among people born in NESB countries than among those born in Australia and other English-speaking countries (AESB). This implies a higher cost per capita.

Assuming that the cost differential for each item of social expenditure remains constant over time, and that they are carried across generations, an Australian population made up of an increasing proportion of NESB people and their descendants, other things being equal, would require higher social expenditure. If this were the case, the retarding of the rate of growth of government social expenditure due to the impact of a higher level of NESB immigrants on the age structure of the population could be offset by a higher utilisation of welfare services. This effect would be ameliorated if social expenditure differentials associated with birthplace composition are not carried across generations, that is, in the alternative case that the 'second generation' does not differ from the rest of the population born in Australia in terms of utilisation of government social services.

These two cases are examined using alternative sets of population projections. Case one is such that social expenditure differentials are carried across generations, and involves projections of NESB immigrants and their descendants born in Australia; in this case, all first and later descendants of NESB people are included. This is the approach used in making the population estimates presented in section 8.2. The alternative case is such that the differences in social expenditure per person do not apply to descendants of NESB immigrants. This involves projections of first generation NESB people only. Hence, the two cases imply differences in the proportion of NESB people to the total population. In case two, NESB people represent a lower proportion of the total population than in case one; therefore, with social expenditure differentials constant over time, case two leads to lower social costs compared with case one. The precise method of measuring these social expenditure differentials associated with birthplace composition is described in the following subsection.

10.3.2 Adjusting Expenditure Growth Rates

The problem is to find a way of adjusting the overall rate of growth of each category of social expenditure given a change in the composition of the population and differences between costs for each group.

Let P_A denote the number of AESB people, and P_N the number of NESB people, where P is the aggregate population. Furthermore, let $g = P_N/P$ denote the proportion of NESB people. Consider a particular item of social expenditure, and let c_A and c_N respectively denote the cost per capita for AESB and NESB people in the social expenditure category, with c denoting the overall cost per capita. Then c can be expressed as:

$$c = (c_A P_A + c_N P_N)/P \tag{10.1}$$

$$c = (1 - g) c_A + g c_N \tag{10.2}$$

Suppose that θ represents the proportionate rate of increase in c_A and c_N over time, and γ denotes the proportionate increase in g. The aggregate cost increases to c_1 where:

$$c_1 = (1+\theta)\{1 - g(1+\gamma)c_A + g(1+\theta)c_N\} \tag{10.3}$$

This can be rewritten as:

$$c_1 = (1+\theta)\{c + g\gamma(c_N - c_A)\} \tag{10.4}$$

The proportionate change in overall social expenditure per capita, δ, in the relevant category is given by $(c_1 - c)/c$ which, combining (10.2) and (10.4) is:

$$\delta = (1+\theta)\{1 + g\gamma(c_N - c_A)\} - 1 \tag{10.5}$$

Then defining the term T as:

$$T = 1 + g\gamma(c_N - c_A)/c \tag{10.6}$$

The term δ can be simplified to:

$$\delta = (1+\theta)T - 1 \tag{10.7}$$

If $\gamma = 0$ then $T = 1$ and $\delta = \theta$, otherwise δ depends on T. Let $r = c_A/c_N$ denote the ratio of per capita cost of AESB to NESB. Then T can be rewritten as:

$$T = 1 + \gamma d \tag{10.8}$$

where:

$$d = \frac{1-r}{1+r\left(\frac{1-g}{g}\right)} \tag{10.9}$$

For example, if $r = 1$, or $g = 0$, then $d = 0$.

Although data are not available on c_A and c_N separately, some indication of r, the ratio of c_A to c_N can be obtained. The values of γ and g can be obtained from the population projections. To illustrate, suppose $r = 0.9$, $\theta = 0.02$, $g = 0.16$ and $\gamma = 0.002$. Substituting into (10.9), (10.8) and (10.7) gives $\delta = 0.02004$. This implies that the higher social expenditure costs for

Table 10.8: Ratio of per Capita Cost of AESB to NESB

Age Pension	Other Age	U Ben	Other SS	Health	Ed	Empl
0.612	0.495	0.812	0.944	0.983	1.462	0.812

NESB people would partially offset the effects of immigration on population ageing. If the proportion of NESB people increases to $g = 0.2$, then δ becomes 0.02007. That is, if the total population is made up of a higher proportion of NESB people, there would be an additional increase in social expenditure and, with everything else constant, a higher social expenditure to GDP ratio.

The method therefore involves two main components. The first is the annual proportional increase in the ratio of NESB people to the total population, obtained directly from the population projections. Calculations were made assuming different levels and composition of the migration intake in each case. However, as before, the discussion focuses on a migration level of 80,000 people with 75 per cent NESB and 25 per cent ESB people.

The second component is the ratio of per capita social expenditure costs of AESB people to NESB people, for each expenditure category. Calculations of the ratio of social expenditure per capita of AESB people to NESB people in each social expenditure category were complicated by the lack of social expenditure data on budget allocations for each of the separate population components. As an approximation, data on Social Security payments (DSS, 1995a) were used to calculate the ratios of Age Pension, Other Age Assistance, Unemployment Benefits, and Other Social Security. Ratios for Health and Education expenditures were calculated using data presented in Mathews (1992, pp.64, 87). Per capita costs by birthplace and for each social expenditure category were estimated, and the ratios of per capita costs of AESB to NESB were calculated. Table 10.8 presents the result of these calculations.

Other age assistance includes widow, mature age and disability pensions. Other social security benefits include sole parent allowance, sickness and special benefits. The value of 1.462 for schooling reflects the fact that the majority of schooling of immigrants is completed overseas. However, as second

Table 10.9: Proportional Change in per Capita Expenditure

	Age Pen	Other A	U Ben	Other S	Health	Educ	Empl
Case 1							
80,000	0.0208	0.0212	0.0203	0.0201	0.0200	0.0197	0.0203
125,000	0.0214	0.0222	0.0206	0.0201	0.0200	0.0195	0.0206
170,000	0.0219	0.0229	0.0207	0.0202	0.0201	0.0193	0.0207
Case 2							
80,000	0.0200	0.0199	0.0200	0.0200	0.0200	0.0200	0.0200
125,000	0.0204	0.0206	0.0201	0.0200	0.0200	0.0198	0.0201
170,000	0.0207	0.0211	0.0203	0.0201	0.0200	0.0196	0.0203

generation migrants attend Australian schools, a weighted average is used according to the immigration assumption adopted. In calculating employment costs, a lack of appropriate information on the birthplace ratio of per capita cost for this category meant that the same value as for unemployment benefit was assigned.

Based on the values presented in Table 10.8 as well as on the demographic variables discussed above, the proportionate changes in each social expenditure category due to changes in the ratio of NESB people to total population under alternative immigration assumptions are calculated and presented in Table 10.9. If the population were homogeneous, each of these growth rates would be 0.02, as used in section 10.2. Table 10.9 presents the proportionate changes in social expenditures for each of the two cases described above and for three alternative levels of immigration, these being 80,000, 125,000 and 170,000 people. Immigrants are assumed to be made up of 75 per cent NESB immigrants and 25 per cent ESB immigrants.

Social expenditures change over time for two reasons. The first is productivity, which is assumed to increase at 2 per cent per annum, and the second is a change in the ratio of NESB people to total population. Increases in the ratio of NESB people to total population would add to social costs. As expected, case 2, which assumes the second generation NESB people do not use welfare services at a higher rate than the rest of the population born in Australia, involves lower values than case 1.

Overall, when social expenditure differentials associated with birthplace composition of the population are taken into account, and assuming these differentials remain constant over time, social expenditure may be expected to increase as the proportion of NESB people to total population rises, other things assumed constant. However, this effect is lower when the need for welfare services is not carried across generations.

10.3.3   Social Expenditure Projections

The projections in this section focus on the effect of population decomposition on social expenditure. The two ways in which population decomposition can affect social expenditure have already been discussed. Demographic differences between AESB and NESB people can alter the age structure of the population and therefore affect social expenditure. Section 8.2 showed the extent to which a migrant intake made up of a higher proportion of NESB people reinforces the retarding of the ageing effect due to immigration. However, an Australian population with a higher proportion of NESB people may generate an adverse effect on social expenditure due to a higher rate of use of government social services associated with the birthplace composition of the population. The social expenditure projections presented in Tables 10.10 to 10.12 take into account these two opposite effects in the alternative cases concerning the characteristics of second and later NESB generation people in terms of their utilisation of government social services.

Table 10.10 shows total costs for each social expenditure category and projection period. In case 1, of non-convergence, total social expenditure is projected by 2051 to be 4.7 per cent higher than in the benchmark case. Most of this difference is ascribed to age pension, health, and other social security payments. In case 2, of convergence, the difference compared with the benchmark case is less, at 3.4 per cent. Except for education expenditure, expenditure categories in case 2 are lower than in case 1.

The retarding of the ageing effect due to immigration also increases the size of the labour force and, therefore, gross domestic product. Hence, both social expenditure and GDP are expected to increase, and it is the ratio

Table 10.10: Social Expenditure ($ Millions): Immigration 80,000

	1988	2001	2011	2021	2031	2041	2051
Case 1							
Age Pen	6,963	12,594	18,953	30,128	45,589	62,856	81,017
Other Age	279	552	787	1,230	1,973	2,866	3,818
U Ben.	3,150	4,596	5,959	7,480	9,237	11,511	14,452
Other SS	12,683	19,588	27,270	37,044	48,452	61,299	77,159
Health	16,174	27,276	38,031	54,790	78,242	105,382	135,308
Educat	9,188	11,994	15,037	18,595	23,080	28,865	35,834
Employ	822	1,125	1,440	1,795	2,214	2,789	3,481
Total	49,258	77,725	107,477	151,061	208,788	275,569	351,070
Case 2							
Age Pen	6,963	12,462	18,602	29,330	44,023	60,204	76,970
Other Age	279	543	765	1,181	1,871	2,685	3,533
U Ben	3,150	4,577	5,915	7,400	9,109	11,316	14,161
Other SS	12,683	19,568	27,220	36,948	48,289	61,045	76,779
Health	16,174	27,269	38,014	54,754	78,176	105,272	135,141
Educat	9,188	12,038	15,135	18,770	23,364	29,303	36,482
Employ	822	1,120	1,429	1,775	2,183	2,741	3,410
Total	49,258	77,577	107,081	150,160	207,015	272,566	346,475

between the two which provides the appropriate index of government financial requirements. Table 10.11 shows these ratios for each social expenditure category as well as the aggregate ratio.

The relatively higher utilisation of welfare services exhibited by NESB immigrants is reflected in Table 10.11. These values, particularly those derived in case 1, are generally higher than the ratios obtained in the benchmark case. During the second and third decades respectively of the next century, in case 1, the aggregate social expenditure to GDP ratio is projected to be 0.0031 and 0.0028 higher than in the benchmark case. Much of this difference is due to higher expenditure on aged pensions. However, after 2031 the gap in the aggregate ratio between case 1 and the benchmark case starts to decrease, and by 2051 case 1 shows a slightly lower value than the corresponding figure in the benchmark case. The social expenditure category with the largest change is that of health expenditure, where the retarding of the ageing effect and the health conditions of NESB people translates into health expenditure ratios which are lower than in the benchmark case after 2031. Social expenditure projections in case 1 produce a health expenditure ratio 0.0026 lower than the corresponding benchmark estimate in 2051.

In case 2, the assumption that second generation immigrants do not differ from the rest of the population born in Australia in terms of utilisation of government social services, produces the lowest ratios. Although social expenditure ratios during the first decades of the projection period are still higher than in the benchmark case, the gap is smaller than in case 1. Furthermore, case 2 produces social expenditure ratios which are lower than the corresponding benchmark case values sooner than case 1. By 2051 it is projected that the age pension ratio will be 0.0026 lower than in the benchmark case, health expenditure will be 0.0027 lower, and the aggregate social expenditure ratio will be 0.0049 lower.

Thus, even in the highest cost case where higher utilisation of welfare services exhibited by current NESB generations is inherited by second and later generations, an annual inflow of 80,000 migrants, with 75 per cent of them being born in non-English-speaking countries, does not lead to substantial higher costs in terms of the ratio of social expenditure to GDP. Furthermore,

Table 10.11: Ratio of Social Expenditure to GDP: Immigration 80,000

	1988	2001	2011	2021	2031	2041	2051
Case 1							
Age Pension	0.0288	0.0345	0.0403	0.0513	0.0628	0.0694	0.0716
Other Age A.	0.0012	0.0015	0.0017	0.0021	0.0027	0.0032	0.0034
Unemp. Ben.	0.0130	0.0126	0.0127	0.0127	0.0127	0.0127	0.0128
Other S.S	0.0524	0.0537	0.0580	0.0631	0.0667	0.0677	0.0682
Health	0.0669	0.0747	0.0809	0.0933	0.1078	0.1163	0.1196
Education	0.0380	0.0329	0.0320	0.0317	0.0318	0.0319	0.0317
Employment	0.0034	0.0031	0.0031	0.0031	0.0030	0.0031	0.0031
Aggregate	0.2036	0.2130	0.2288	0.2573	0.2875	0.3042	0.3104
Case 2							
Age Pension	0.0288	0.0341	0.0396	0.0500	0.0606	0.0665	0.0681
Other Age A.	0.0012	0.0015	0.0016	0.0020	0.0026	0.0030	0.0031
Unemp. Ben.	0.0130	0.0125	0.0126	0.0126	0.0125	0.0125	0.0125
Other S.S	0.0524	0.0536	0.0579	0.0629	0.0665	0.0674	0.0679
Health	0.0669	0.0747	0.0809	0.0933	0.1077	0.1162	0.1195
Education	0.0380	0.0330	0.0322	0.0320	0.0322	0.0324	0.0323
Employment	0.0034	0.0031	0.0030	0.0030	0.0030	0.0030	0.0030
Aggregate	0.2036	0.2126	0.2279	0.2558	0.2851	0.3009	0.3064

if the social and economic circumstances that make first generation immigrants use social services more intensively than people born in Australia are not carried accross generations, immigration can reduce the rate of growth of social expenditure.

As in the benchmark case, taking into account the population composition and social expenditure differentials, higher levels of immigration may retard the growth of the ratio of social expenditure to GDP, as shown in Table 10.12. Increasing the level of annual immigration from 80,000 to 125,000 people is projected to restrain the growth in the social expenditure ratio from 0.3104 to 0.3035 in case 1, and to 0.2983 in case 2, by the year 2051. Further reductions are achieved with 170,000 immigrants per year.

However, higher immigration levels lead to a higher proportion of NESB people in the total population. This affects social expenditure. Thus, comparing these results with the benchmark case, the difference in the social

Table 10.12: Social Expenditure Ratios and Immigration

Immigration	1988	2001	2011	2021	2031	2041	2051
Case 1							
80,000	0.2036	0.2130	0.2288	0.2573	0.2875	0.3042	0.3104
125,000	0.2036	0.2119	0.2256	0.2515	0.2796	0.2962	0.3035
170,000	0.2036	0.2107	0.2227	0.2462	0.2728	0.2897	0.2981
Case 2							
80,000	0.2036	0.2126	0.2279	0.2558	0.2851	0.3009	0.3064
125,000	0.2036	0.2113	0.2245	0.2495	0.2765	0.2920	0.2983
170,000	0.2036	0.2101	0.2214	0.2440	0.2693	0.2849	0.2921

expenditure ratio increases with the immigration level; see Tables 10.12 and 10.6. For example, by 2031, while an immigration level of 80,000 people is projected to produce an aggregate ratio which is 0.0028 higher in case 1 than the corresponding value in the benchmark case, an annual intake of 125,000 produces a ratio 0.0049 higher, and immigration of 170,000 translates into an aggregate social expenditure ratio 0.0063 higher than the figure for the corresponding benchmark case. Those differences are lower in case 2. Nevertheless, even in the highest cost case, the impact on the social expenditure ratio due to substantial increases in immigration flows is not as large as might be expected in view of the relatively higher utilisation of social services exhibited by current first generation migrants.

Chapter 11

A Stochastic Approach

Social expenditure projections rely heavily on assumptions about a large number of variables such as future labour force participation rates, unemployment rates, and productivity growth. No attempt has been made to examine the extent to which projected increases in the ratio of expenditure to national income are statistically significant, or even whether any bias is imparted because of the large uncertainty surrounding many of the variables. At the most, a few sensitivity analyses have been carried out by considering, as with population projections, high and low values of some of the variables; see Creedy and Taylor (1993a) for examples.

The aim of this chapter is to examine the statistical properties of social expenditure projections with the use of a stochastic model. The approach is based on the specification of distributions of the relevant variables involved in the calculation of expenditure ratios. The resulting 'sampling distribution' of the social expenditure ratio cannot be derived analytically, so simulation methods are used to produce numerical results. The issue is how the variability in the component variables translates to variability in the projections. Can the method of producing standard projections be regarded as providing unbiased estimates of the mean of the sampling distribution of expenditure ratios? Are projected increases in the ratio likely to be statistically significantly different? It is also of interest to know whether there are certain variables which contribute relatively more than others to the sampling variation.

Section 11.1 briefly presents what is referred to as the deterministic model used to produce standard projections. Section 11.2 presents the stochastic model in which the values of a wide range of variables are treated as being drawn from specified distributions. Section 11.3 presents some results of simulation analyses. The assumption is made that each variable is normally distributed, and the use of the lognormal distribution is examined in section 11.4.

11.1   A Deterministic Model

This section describes the deterministic model used to make projections of the ratio of social expenditure to gross domestic product. Separate projections of social expenditure and GDP are described below. The method is described in more detail in chapter 7. In addition to the many assumptions which are required to make projections, there are many potential interdependencies which are not easy to model. For example, productivity itself may depend on social expenditures and the age distribution of workers. Furthermore, participation rates and population growth are to some extent interdependent. These factors can be borne in mind when selecting the values of variables to be used in making the projections, although they are not modelled explicitly.

11.1.1   Social Expenditure

The population is divided into N age groups and the numbers in each group at time t are placed in a vector p_t. This is divided into male and female age distributions, where $p_t = p_{m,t} + p_{f,t}$. The per capita social expenditures per year within each group are placed in a matrix with N rows and k columns, where there are k items of social expenditure. If this matrix is denoted S, then the element s_{ij} measures the per capita cost of the jth type of social expenditure in the ith age group. Suppose that the jth type of social expenditure per capita is expected to grow in real terms at the annual rate ψ_j in each age group. Then define g_t as the column vector whose jth element is equal to $(1 + \psi_j)^{t-1}$, for $j = 1, ..., k$. Aggregate social expenditure at time t, C_t, is thus equal to:

$$C_t = g_t' S' p \qquad (11.1)$$

where the dash indicates transposition. This could be extended by allowing for expenditure per person in each category and age to differ for males and females, but such information is rarely available.

11.1.2 Gross Domestic Product

Projections of Gross Domestic Product (GDP) depend on assumptions about five factors: initial productivity, defined as GDP per employed person, productivity growth, employment rates, participation rates and the population of working age. Total employment is the product of the population, participation rates and the employment rate. Employment is calculated by multiplying the labour utilisation rate by the labour force. If U_t is the total unemployment rate in period t, the utilisation rate is $1 - U_t$. The aggregate unemployment rate is calculated by dividing the total number of unemployed persons in period t, V_t, by the total labour force in that period, L_t. The value of V_t is in turn calculated by multiplying the age distribution of unemployment rates by the age distribution of the labour force, where these differ according to both age and sex. Let the vectors U_m and U_f be the N-element age distributions of male and female unemployment rates. If the symbol $\hat{\ }$ represents diagonalisation, whereby the vector is written as the leading diagonal of a square matrix with other elements equal to zero, the total number of people unemployed in period t is;

$$V_t = U_{m,t}' \widehat{L}_{m,t} p_{m,t} + U_{f,t}' \widehat{L}_{f,t} p_{f,t} \qquad (11.2)$$

The labour force in period t is given by:

$$L_t = L_{m,t}' p_{m,t} + L_{f,t}' p_{f,t} \qquad (11.3)$$

It is possible to express GDP in period t as the product of the utilisation rate, $1 - U_t$, equal to $1 - V_t/L_t$, the labour force, L_t, and productivity. Suppose productivity grows at the constant rate, δ. Hence:

$$GDP_t = \left\{ \frac{GDP_1}{(1 - U_1) L_1} \right\} (1 + \delta)^{t-1} (1 - U_t) L_t \qquad (11.4)$$

If the population age distribution, along with the sex and age specific participation and unemployment rates, are constant, then the social expenditure to GDP ratio remains constant if all items of expenditure grow at the same rate as productivity; that is if $\delta = \psi_j$, for $j = 1, ..., k$.

11.2   A Stochastic Model

The various unemployment and participation rates and growth rates of productivity and social expenditure costs cannot be known with certainty. One way to allow for this uncertainty is to specify, for each appropriate variable, a distribution. Each observation is regarded as being drawn from the corresponding distribution. A large number of projections can be made, where each projection uses random drawings from each of the distributions. This exercise produces a sampling distribution of the ratio of social expenditure to GDP. This type of numerical simulation needs to be carried out in view of the complexity of the relevant transformation required to obtain the social expenditure ratio, given by (11.1) divided by (11.4), which rules out the derivation of the precise functional form of its distribution.

11.2.1   Distributional Specification

It is first necessary to specify the form of the various distributions and a procedure for calibrating their parameters, in view of the fact that conventional estimates cannot be obtained. Suppose that a relevant variable, x, which may be an unemployment rate or item of social expenditure, is assumed to be normally distributed with mean and variance μ and σ^2 respectively, so that x is $N(\mu, \sigma^2)$. If v represents a random drawing from the standard normal distribution $N(0, 1)$, a simulated value of x can be obtained using:

$$x = \mu + v\sigma \qquad (11.5)$$

since $(x - \mu)/\sigma$ is $N(0,1)$. It is possible in principle for this method to generate negative values of x, although in practice it can be avoided. However, the use of the lognormal distribution, where all values are positive, gives very similar results: this is discussed in section 11.4.

The value of μ may be based on the current observed value. The problem arises, however, of how to specify an appropriate order of magnitude for σ^2, given that direct estimates cannot be obtained. A natural approach is to specify a range containing a given proportion of values. For example, it may be thought that $100(2q - 1)$ per cent of values lie in the range $\mu(1 \pm \theta_q)$; hence if $q = 0.975$ and θ_q is thought to be 0.10, then 95 per cent, given by 100 times $\{(2)(0.975) - 1\}$, of values are assumed to lie in the range with a lower limit of 10 per cent less than the arithmetic mean and an upper limit of 10 per cent above the mean. This can be converted into a statement about σ as follows.

From tables of the standard normal distribution, it is a simple matter to obtain the value of the qth percentile of the distribution, v_q, corresponding to any given value of q. For example, $v_{0.975}$ is equal to 1.96; so 95 per cent of values lie in the range $\mu(1 \pm 1.96)$, or 95 per cent of values lie in a range given by 1.96 standard deviations either side of the mean. Hence, the upper limit of this range, given by $\mu(1 + \theta_q)$, is equal to $\mu + v_q\sigma$. Setting these equal and rearranging gives the required value of σ expressed as a function of the other variables:

$$\sigma = \mu\left(\frac{\theta_q}{v_q}\right) \qquad (11.6)$$

For a specified arthmetic mean, μ, the substitution of (11.6) into (11.5) shows that a random value of x, associated with the random $N(0,1)$ variable, v, is given by:

$$x = \mu\left\{1 + \theta_q\left(\frac{v}{v_q}\right)\right\} \qquad (11.7)$$

The above approach makes it possible to allow for variability in all of the labour force participation rates and unemployment rates, along with all the social expenditure costs for each age group and category, by specifying a relatively small number of values of θ_q. For example, a single value of θ_q can be applied to each of the male unemployment rates, rather than imposing a difference value for each of the N age groups. Nevertheless, the variance of the unemployment rate differs among age groups because of the relationship in (11.6). Similarly, a single value of θ_q can be used to describe the variability in Nk social expenditure costs, where each item has a different variance depending on its value of μ. Simulations are therefore reported below using the following seven values of θ_q: $\theta_{mu}, \theta_{mp}, \theta_{fu}, \theta_{fp}, \theta_s, \theta_\delta, \theta_\psi$, where the subscript mu refers to male unemployment rates, mp refers to male participation rates, and so on, and s refers to social expenditure categories.

11.2.2   Joint Distributions

It may be thought that some variables are jointly distributed. In particular, it seems useful to allow for the possibility that there is some correlation between the growth rate of productivity, δ, and the growth rate of one of the items of social expenditure, ψ_j. Suppose that δ and ψ are distributed as:

$$N\left(\delta, \psi | \mu_\delta, \mu_\psi, \sigma_\delta^2, \sigma_\psi^2, \rho\right) \qquad (11.8)$$

where ρ is the correlation coefficient. A random drawing of δ can be obtained using, as above:

$$\delta = \mu_\delta + v\sigma_\delta \qquad (11.9)$$

where again v is an $N(0,1)$ variable. Then a drawing from the distribution of ψ can be obtained by selecting from the conditional distribution of ψ for given δ. Using the standard result that:

$$F\left(\psi | \delta\right) \text{ is } N\left(\mu_\psi + \rho\frac{\sigma_\psi}{\sigma_\delta}\left(\delta - \mu_\delta\right), \sigma_\psi^2\left(1 - \rho^2\right)\right) \qquad (11.10)$$

If v represents another random drawing from a standard normal distribution, then a value of ψ is obtained using;

$$\psi = \mu_\psi + \rho\frac{\sigma_\psi}{\sigma_\delta}\left(\delta - \mu_\delta\right) + v\sigma_\psi\sqrt{1 - \rho^2} \qquad (11.11)$$

Table 11.1: Population Projections 2001 to 2021

	2001		2011		2021	
	M	F	M	F	M	F
0-15	1883.5	1803.0	1856.9	1786.2	1854.2	1782.6
16-24	1329.8	1267.7	1391.1	1335.5	1381.1	1334.6
25-39	2158.5	2124.0	2098.4	2035.3	2154.4	2099.2
40-49	1409.5	1418.0	1483.8	1477.7	1433.2	1394.9
50-59	1178.5	1163.6	1369.9	1396.9	1448.0	1457.5
60-64	412.7	410.0	591.6	612.2	673.6	706.4
65-69	325.6	343.2	468.9	494.0	567.8	622.8
70-74	287.3	324.2	329.3	364.3	479.9	546.0
75+	450.4	703.0	516.8	792.1	681.0	993.7

In the following simulations, the same correlation coefficient, ρ, is used for each of the social expenditure categories.

11.3 Simulation Results

This section presents simulation results for projections of the ratio of social expenditure to GDP in Australia up to the year 2051. The social expenditure costs, along with the male and female age-specific labour force participation and unemployment rates, are taken from chapter 10. The male and female age distributions used in each of the prediction years are given in Tables 11.1 and 11.2. These values are used to specify the corresponding values of the arithmetic means of the various distributions. The population projections are made on the basis of an assumed constant flow of immigrants of 80,000 per year.

It should be stressed that the results are for illustrative purposes only, with emphasis being placed on the statistical properties of the resulting distributions. The precise results obviously depend on the assumptions made regarding the various values of θ, which reflect views regarding the underlying distributions. Direct observations cannot be used to produce standard statistical estimates, so that a degree of judgement is always required. In order to provide a 'benchmark' illustrative case, the value of each of the θs

Table 11.2: Population Projections 2031 to 2051 (000s)

	2031		2041		2051	
	M	F	M	F	M	F
0-15	1895.7	1821.8	1893.6	1819.3	1903.3	1828.3
16-24	1365.3	1318.2	1401.9	1352.6	1403.7	1353.7
25-39	2170.9	2129.8	2139.8	2098.4	2178.9	2134.4
40-49	1466.3	1428.9	1501.5	1475.7	1470.6	1444.4
50-59	1403.8	1378.2	1441.6	1413.9	1480.3	1461.7
60-64	708.2	725.5	656.0	658.3	695.5	695.8
65-69	613.9	664.5	633.8	659.4	639.5	660.1
70-74	555.9	633.3	593.8	653.9	557.6	596.2
75+	937.0	1377.2	1131.8	1699.3	1262.4	1864.0

Table 11.3: Benchmark Ratios of Social Expenditure to GDP

	2001	2011	2021	2031	2041	2051
Projection	0.211	0.226	0.254	0.285	0.303	0.311
5th percent	0.203	0.214	0.238	0.261	0.274	0.276
Lower Q	0.208	0.221	0.247	0.275	0.291	0.296
Median	0.211	0.226	0.254	0.285	0.303	0.311
Upper Q	0.215	0.231	0.261	0.295	0.316	0.327
95th percent	0.221	0.239	0.273	0.311	0.336	0.352
Standard deviation	0.005	0.007	0.011	0.015	0.019	0.023
(95th - Med)/Med	0.045	0.057	0.074	0.091	0.110	0.130
(Med - 5th)/Med	0.041	0.051	0.065	0.082	0.097	0.114
Median + 1.96 SD	0.222	0.241	0.275	0.314	0.341	0.357
Median - 1.96 SD	0.200	0.211	0.233	0.255	0.265	0.266

was set equal to 0.10 for q equal to 0.975, so that v_q is in each case equal to 1.96. Hence 95 per cent of values of each variable were assumed to lie in a range enclosed by $\mu(1 \pm 0.10)$. The value of ρ was set equal to zero. In this benchmark case, the growth of productivity was set equal to 0.02, along with the assumed growth in the per capita cost of each item of social expenditure. The aggregate increase in social expenditure to GDP ratio therefore arises predominantly from population ageing.

Summary measures obtained using the benchmark assumptions are given in Table 11.3, for which 5,000 simulations were carried out. The first row

Table 11.4: Alternative Values of θ

θ	0.3	0.2	0.1	0.01	0.005	0.003
$\rho = 0$						
Mean:	0.29033	0.28718	0.28530	0.28468	0.28468	0.28468
SD:	0.04654	0.03051	0.01510	0.00158	0.00064	0.00030
Median:	0.28650	0.28540	0.28480	0.28467	0.28467	0.28467
$\rho = 0.1$						
Mean:	0.28893	0.28677	0.28525	0.28468	0.28468	0.28468
SD:	0.03727	0.02649	0.01412	0.00151	0.00071	0.00031
Median:	0.28616	0.28523	0.28472	0.28466	0.28467	0.28467

of the table gives the value of the ratio of social expenditure to GDP that
is obtained by the standard 'deterministic' approach. This suggests that
population ageing in Australia will rise from just over 20 per cent of GDP
to just over 30 per cent, unless various policy changes are made in order to
reduce social costs per capita. The next ten rows of the table give summary
measures of the sampling distribution produced from the 5,000 simulations.

The first point to note is that the median is in each case very close to
the projected value, and the same is true of the arithmetic mean values (not
reported in the table). The deterministic projection method seems therefore
to produce unbiased projections. The dispersion of the sampling distribution
increases with the length of the projection period, as expected. The distributions are not entirely symmetrical, as seen from the proportional deviations
of the 5th and 95 percentiles from the median, although the extent of the
asymmetry is small. It does, however, increase slightly as the projection period increases. The final two rows of Table 11.3 can be used to produce 95
per cent 'confidence intervals' of the projected social expenditure ratios. It
can be seen that the changes over any ten year period are not statistically
significant. However, the increase from 2001 to 2021 is significant, and the
increase from 2011 to 2051 is significant.

A histogram of the distribution of the ratio of social expenditure to GDP
for 2031, using the benchmark assumptions, is shown in Figure 11.1. This
shows the approximate symmetry of the distribution.

The result of varying the (common) value of θ is shown in Table 11.4,

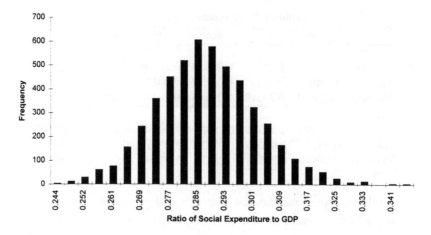

Figure 11.1: Distribution of Social Expenditure Ratio 2031

which gives results for the year 2031. The first part of the table is, as in
the benchmark case, for $\rho = 0$, whereas the second part of the table is for a
value of ρ of 0.10 for the correlation coefficient between each growth rate of
social expenditure per capita and the growth rate of productivity. Table 11.4
clearly demonstrates how the sampling distribution gradually 'collapses' on
the projected value as the value of θ falls. The positive correlation between
the relevant growth rates produces a lower standard deviation of the sampling
distribution, or standard error, in the earlier projection periods, but a slightly
higher value in the later periods.

In order to investigate the effects of greater uncertainty in particular
variables, simulations were carried out in which one value of θ was an increase
above the benchmark value of 0.10. The results are shown in Tables 11.5 to
11.9, for unemployment rates, participation rates, social expenditure costs
per capita, productivity growth and finally the growth rate of the social
expenditure costs, assumed, as above, to be the same for each item. Each
table is for a value of $\rho = 0$.

It can be seen that the higher variability in unemployment rates of males
and females has little effect on the sampling properties of the projections.

Table 11.5: Unemployment Rate

	2001	2011	2021	2031	2041	2051
5th percent	0.203	0.214	0.237	0.261	0.274	0.276
Lower Q	0.208	0.221	0.247	0.275	0.291	0.297
Median	0.211	0.226	0.254	0.285	0.303	0.311
Upper Q	0.215	0.231	0.262	0.295	0.316	0.327
95th percent	0.221	0.239	0.273	0.311	0.336	0.352
Standard deviation	0.005	0.007	0.011	0.015	0.019	0.023
(95th - Med)/Med	0.046	0.058	0.073	0.091	0.110	0.130
(Med - 5th)/Med	0.041	0.051	0.066	0.082	0.097	0.114
Median + 1.96 SD	0.222	0.241	0.275	0.314	0.341	0.357
Median - 1.96 SD	0.200	0.211	0.233	0.255	0.265	0.266

Table 11.6: Participation Rate

	2001	2011	2021	2031	2041	2051
5th percent	0.198	0.210	0.234	0.258	0.271	0.274
Lower Q	0.206	0.219	0.245	0.273	0.290	0.296
Median	0.211	0.226	0.254	0.285	0.303	0.312
Upper Q	0.217	0.233	0.264	0.297	0.318	0.329
95th percent	0.227	0.244	0.278	0.316	0.342	0.356
Standard deviation	0.009	0.010	0.013	0.017	0.021	0.025
(95th - Med)/Med	0.074	0.080	0.092	0.108	0.126	0.143
(Med - 5th)/Med	0.065	0.070	0.080	0.093	0.107	0.121
Median + 1.96 SD	0.229	0.246	0.280	0.319	0.346	0.361
Median - 1.96 SD	0.194	0.206	0.228	0.250	0.261	0.262

Table 11.7: Social Expenditure Cost

	2001	2011	2021	2031	2041	2051
5th percent	0.201	0.213	0.236	0.259	0.272	0.274
Lower Q	0.207	0.220	0.246	0.274	0.290	0.296
Median	0.211	0.226	0.254	0.285	0.303	0.311
Upper Q	0.216	0.232	0.263	0.296	0.317	0.328
95th percent	0.223	0.241	0.275	0.313	0.339	0.354
Standard deviation	0.007	0.009	0.012	0.016	0.021	0.024
(95th - Med)/Med	0.056	0.066	0.080	0.099	0.118	0.138
(Med - 5th)/Med	0.051	0.059	0.073	0.089	0.104	0.119
Median + 1.96 SD	0.225	0.243	0.278	0.317	0.344	0.360
Median - 1.96 SD	0.198	0.209	0.231	0.253	0.263	0.263

Table 11.8: Productivity Growth

	2001	2011	2021	2031	2041	2051
5th percent	0.200	0.208	0.226	0.245	0.253	0.251
Lower Q	0.207	0.218	0.242	0.268	0.282	0.285
Median	0.211	0.226	0.254	0.285	0.303	0.312
Upper Q	0.216	0.234	0.266	0.302	0.327	0.340
95th percent	0.224	0.246	0.286	0.330	0.363	0.386
Standard deviation	0.007	0.012	0.018	0.026	0.034	0.041
(95th - Med)/Med	0.059	0.089	0.124	0.161	0.198	0.239
(Med - 5th)/Med	0.054	0.080	0.109	0.137	0.165	0.195
Median + 1.96 SD	0.226	0.250	0.290	0.336	0.370	0.393
Median - 1.96 SD	0.197	0.203	0.219	0.233	0.237	0.230

Table 11.9: Social Expenditure Growth

	2001	2011	2021	2031	2041	2051
5th percent	0.202	0.213	0.234	0.256	0.267	0.268
Lower Q	0.207	0.220	0.246	0.273	0.289	0.294
Median	0.211	0.226	0.254	0.285	0.304	0.313
Upper Q	0.215	0.232	0.263	0.298	0.321	0.333
95th percent	0.222	0.242	0.277	0.318	0.347	0.366
Standard deviation	0.006	0.009	0.013	0.019	0.024	0.029
(95th - Med)/Med	0.050	0.068	0.090	0.115	0.142	0.168
(Med - 5th)/Med	0.043	0.060	0.080	0.102	0.122	0.143
Median + 1.96 SD	0.223	0.243	0.280	0.322	0.352	0.371
Median - 1.96 SD	0.200	0.209	0.229	0.249	0.257	0.255

However, the increase in the dispersion of participation rates initially has a large effect on the standard error, although this increases at a slower rate than in the benchmark case, so that by 2051 they are similar. The largest change, from the benchmark case, is observed when θ_δ, which relates to the growth rate of productivity, is increased; this is shown in Table 11.8.

The near symmetry of the sampling distributions, and the unbiased nature of the standard projections, may be thought to arise from the assumption that each of the relevant variables is normally distributed. However, given the complexity of the transformation between the ratio of social expenditure to GDP and the various components, it is far from obvious that this result would arise.

11.4 The Lognormal Distribution

Instead of assuming that the relevant variables are normally distributed, suppose that they are lognormal, so that x is $\Lambda\left(\mu, \sigma^2\right)$. Suppose that $100(2q-1)$ per cent of values of the logarithms of x are throught to be in the range $(1 \pm \theta_q)\log x$. Then, as above, $\{\mu\left(1+\theta_q\right)-\mu\}/\sigma = v_q$ and $\sigma = \mu\theta_q/v_q$. In this case it is possible to have negative values of μ where the median is less than 1, so that it is appropriate to use the absolute value of $\mu\theta_q/v_q$.

Suppose, as above, that the arithmetic mean value of x, $\bar{x}$, is known, based, say, on the current value. In this case it is necessary to derive both the mean and the variance of logarithms. From the property of the lognormal distribution it is known that $\bar{x} = \exp\left(\mu + \sigma^2/2\right)$. Substituting for σ^2 into this expression gives:

$$\log \bar{x} = \mu + \frac{\mu^2}{2}\left(\frac{\theta_q}{v_q}\right)^2 \tag{11.12}$$

This gives a quadratic in μ, the roots of which are given by:

$$\frac{-1 \pm \sqrt{1 + 2\left(\frac{\theta_q}{v_q}\right)^2 \log \bar{x}}}{\left(\frac{\theta_q}{v_q}\right)^2} \tag{11.13}$$

Although there are typically two distinct roots, it is appropriate to take
the value of μ closest to $\log \bar{x}$. Indeed, the other root is usually obviously
inappropriate. The appropriate value of μ can then be used to obtain the
required value of σ. A random value of x, corresponding to a random normal
variate, v, is then given by:

$$x = \exp\left(\mu + v\sigma\right) \tag{11.14}$$

The lognormal has the advantage that the values are automatically con-
strained to be positive.

Care must be taken in the choice of θ_q in the lognormal case. For example,
if $\bar{x} = 100$, the use of $\theta_q = 0.10$ gives, in the normal distribution case, a range
from 90 to 110 which is specified to contain $100(2q - 1)$ per cent of values.
In the lognormal case $(1 \pm 0.10) \log 100$ translates into a range of values of x
from 63.096 to 158.49, which is much too large. Suppose it is desired to have
similar upper bounds in the normal and lognormal cases. This means that a
given value of θ_q in the normal case, say θ_N, translates into a corresponding
value in the lognormal case of θ_Λ, where:

$$\exp\left\{(1 + \theta_\Lambda) \log \bar{x}\right\} = (1 + \theta_N)\,\bar{x}$$

so that:

$$\theta_\Lambda = \frac{\log\left(1 + \theta_N\right)}{\log \bar{x}} \tag{11.15}$$

Notice that if $\bar{x} < 1$ the value of θ_Λ corresponding to any θ_N is negative.
This also ensures that the value of σ is suitably positive.

The distribution of the ratio of social expenditure to GDP for 2031, using
the benchmark assumptions, is shown for the lognormal case in Figure 11.2.
This shows that, despite the lognormality of the many component distributions the distribution of the ratio is again approximately symmetric.

The results of this chapter suggest that while the deterministic approach
generates unbiased values, these may be associated with quite large standard errors. In making projections, it is therefore recommended that serious

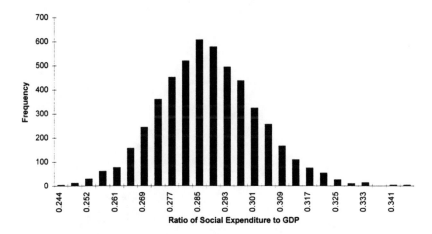

Figure 11.2: Distribution for 2031: Lognormal Case

consideration should be given to the likely variability in the component distributions. In particular, it was found that the results are relatively more sensitive to the assumed growth rate of productivity.

Chapter 12

Conclusions

This book has been concerned with the implications of population ageing in Australia for the ratio of social expenditure to GDP. In this context, immigration can play an important role because it slows down the extent of population ageing. The demographic effects of immigration depend on the size of the intake as well as on fertility, mortality and the age structure of immigrants. Large inflows of people with higher fertility and a younger age structure than the native population can retard the process of population ageing and therefore also the growth in the ratio of social expenditure to GDP. However, the impact of immigration on the ratio of social expenditure to GDP is not restricted to its demographic effects. Differences in social and economic characteristics between immigrants and the native population may alter the propensity to use social services and hence the level of social expenditure per capita in each age group.

The approach used in this book has allowed for this double impact of immigration on the ratio of social expenditure to GDP. The method used allows for variations in the birthplace composition of the population as well as the demographic and socio-economic characteristics associated with each population component.

Comparing the demographic and socio-economic characteristics of the three birthplace groupings of the Australian population, namely, people born in Australia, people born in other English-speaking background countries (ESB), and those from non-English-speaking background countries (NESB), it was observed that differences between these birthplace groupings were particularly marked when comparing NESB immigrants with people born in Australia. The characteristics exhibited by ESB people were closer to people born in Australia than to NESB people. The Australian resident population was thus redefined as being made up of two groups. The first group consists of those born in Australia and in other English-speaking background countries, and are referred to as AESB. The second group consists of NESB people and their descendants. This redefinition of the Australian population was used to project population and social expenditure under the population decomposition approach.

The results of the study suggest that immigration can retard population ageing to some extent. For example, under the benchmark case, annual immigration of 80,000 persons reduces the proportion of those aged 65 years and over by 1.1 percentage points by 2031, compared with an immigration level of 40,000 people per year. With 170,000 immigrants the proportion of people in that age group decreases by 3.1 percentage points.

This retarding of the ageing effect is particularly influenced by the age structure of the migrant intake. Thus, comparing the population age structure derived from an intake of migrants, of whom 59 per cent are younger than 30 years, with the age structure of the population that would result from an intake with 80 per cent less than 30 years, it was found that by the year 2031, the younger intake of 80,000 immigrants per year increases the percentage of the population aged between 1 and 39 years by 1.9 percentage points and reduces the percentage of people older than 65 by 1.1 percentage points.

Similarly, the retarding of the ageing effect is accentuated when account is taken of the demographic differences associated with birthplace composition of the population. Thus, in making projections with population decomposition, an intake of 80,000 people with 75 per cent of them assumed to have the demographic characteristics of migrants born in NESB countries, it was found that by 2031 the proportion of people younger than 40 years increases by 1 percentage point compared with a similar immigration level in the benchmark case.

As with the population projections, the social expenditure to GDP ratio was projected under the traditional assumption, which ignores the composition of the population, and under the alternative approach of population decomposition. The benchmark social expenditure projections focused on the effects of the changing population age structure on social expenditure. It was found that, as the population ages, education spending as a proportion of GDP decreases, while the age pension, other age assistance, and health ratios increase. The aggregate social expenditure ratio increases due to the fact that expenditure per capita on old people is much higher than for younger age groups.

Higher levels of immigration retard the growth of the social expenditure to GDP ratio. Thus, by 2031, immigration of 40,000 people is projected to produce a social expenditure to GDP ratio of 0.2956, whereas increasing the annual intake to 170,000 is projected to produce a ratio of 0.2665. In the case of 40,000 immigrants, the ratio of social expenditure to GDP is projected to grow by 29 per cent between 2011 and 2031, but with 170,000 immigrants that ratio is projected to grow at the lower rate of 22 per cent over the same period.

As expected, a migrant intake with a younger age structure accentuates the slowing down of the rate of growth of social expenditure. For example, with the age structure of the intake of migrants to Australia between 1988-89 and 1992-93, the social expenditure to GDP ratio is projected to be 0.2921 by the year 2051 if 170,000 immigrants settle in Australia each year of the projection period. A similar social expenditure to GDP ratio would be achieved with only half that intake of migrants but with an increase in the participation of people younger than 30 years from 59 per cent to 80 per cent of the total annual intake.

Under the population decomposition approach, two forces are at play when projecting the social expenditure ratio. On the one hand, the retarding of population ageing effect can be expected to produce lower social expenditure ratios. On the other hand, social expenditure differentials associated with population decomposition, whereby an Australian population with a higher proportion of NESB people and their descendants can generate higher rates of growth in social expenditure, have the potential to increase the ratio of social expenditure to GDP. These effects were analysed for two alternative cases: case 1 assumed that social expenditure differentials between AESB and NESB people remained constant across generations, whereas case 2 assumed that second generation immigrants do not differ from the rest of the population born in Australia in terms of utilisation of government social services.

It was found that total social expenditure, in dollar terms, increases when demographic and socio-economic differences associated with birthplace are taken into account. However, the retarding of the ageing effect due to immigration also increases the size of the labour force and therefore also total output. Hence, both social expenditure and GDP are expected to increase and, according to the results obtained in this study, GDP is projected to increase by more than social expenditure leading to a reduction in the overall social expenditure ratio. As expected, the ratio obtained in case 2 was lower than in case 1.

Thus, under the assumptions adopted in this book, immigration has the potential to restrain the rate of growth of the social expenditure to GDP ratio. Even in the high cost case that higher utilisation of welfare services exhibited by current NESB generations is inherited by second and later generations, it is projected that higher proportions of NESB people have very little effect on the ratio of social expenditure to GDP.

This book has necessarily concentrated on the effects of population ageing, with the associated role of immigration, on social expenditure. There is a major positive conclusion, that immigration can reduce the growth of the ratio of social expenditure to GDP, and a negative conclusion, that the birthplace composition of immigrants has a negligible effect on the projections. In the wider debate on social expenditure and population ageing, it should of course be remembered that there are many other factors to be taken into consideration. In particular, projections appear to be more sensitive to changes in productivity growth, participation and unemployment rates than to changes in immigration levels and the age structure.

Bibliography

[1] Aaron, H. (1966) The Social Insurance Paradox. *Canadian Journal of Economics*, 32, pp. 371-379.

[2] Ablett, J. (1994) Generational Accounting and the Contribution of Migrants to the Public Purse in Australia. *The University of New South Wales School of Economics Discussion Paper.*

[3] Ablett, J. (1996) Generational Accounting - An Australian Perspective. *Review of Income and Wealth*, 42, pp. 91-105.

[4] Ackland, R. and Williams, L. (1992) *Immigrants and the Australian Labour Market: the Experience of Three Recessions.* Canberra: BIPR, AGPS.

[5] Ahlburg, D. and Vaupel, J. (1990) Alternative Projections of the US Population. *Demography*, 27, pp. 639-652.

[6] Atkinson, M. and Creedy, J. (1997) The Choice of Early Retirement Age and the Australian Superannuation System. *Australian Journal of Labour Economics* (forthcoming).

[7] Auerbach, A.J., Gokhale, J. and Kotlikoff, L.J. (1994) Generational Accounting: A Meaningful Way to Evaluate Fiscal Policy. *Journal of Economic Perspectives*, 8, pp. 73-94.

[8] Australian Bureau of Statistics (1989a) *Projections of the Population of Australia States and Territories 1989 to 2031* (Cat. no. 3222.0). Canberra: AGPS.

[9] Australian Bureau of Statistics (1989b) *Overseas Born Australians 1988, A Statistical Profile* (Cat. no. 4112.0). Canberra: AGPS.

[10] Australian Bureau of Statistics (1989c) *Estimated Resident Population by Sex and Age: States and Territories of Australia, June 1988 and Preliminary June 1989* (Cat. no. 3201.0). Canberra: AGPS.

[11] Australian Bureau of Statistics (1990) *Survey of Income and Housing Costs and Amenities, Australia* (Cat. no. 6523.0). Canberra: AGPS.

[12] Australian Bureau of Statistics (1993a) *Survey of Disability, Ageing and Carers*. Canberra: AGPS.

[13] Australian Bureau of Statistics (1993b) *Survey of Education and Training*. Data on magnetic media.

[14] Australian Bureau of Statistics (1994a) *Estimated Resident Population by Country of Birth, Age and Sex, Preliminary June 1993*. Data on magnetic media.

[15] Australian Bureau of Statistics (1994b) *Australian Social Trends* (Cat. no. 4102.0). Canberra: AGPS.

[16] Australian Bureau of Statistics, Queensland (1994c) *The Social Characteristics of Immigrants in Australia*. Canberra: BIPR, AGPS.

[17] Australian Bureau of Statistics (1994d) *Australia's Long-term Unemployed, A Statistical Profile* (Cat. no. 6255.0). Canberra: AGPS.

[18] Australian Bureau of Statistics (1994e) *Labour Force Status and Other Characteristics of Migrants, Australia, September 1993* (Cat. no. 6250.0). Canberra: AGPS.

[19] Australian Bureau of Statistics (1994f) *Training and Education Experience, Australia, 1993* (Cat. no. 6278.0). Canberra: AGPS.

[20] Australian Bureau of Statistics (1994g) *The Labour Force Australia* (Cat. no. 6203.0). Canberra: AGPS.

[21] Australian Bureau of Statistics (1995) *Caring in Families: Support for Persons Who Are Older or Have Disabilities* (Cat. no. 4423.0). Canberra: AGPS.

[22] Australian Bureau of Statistics (1996a) *Year Book Australia 1996* (Cat. No. 1301.0). Canberra: AGPS.

[23] Australian Bureau of Statistics (1996b) *Australian Social Trends 1996* (Cat no. 4102.0). Canberra: AGPS.

[24] Australian Institute of Health and Welfare (AIHW) (1995) *Australia's Welfare 1995: Services and Assistance*. Canberra: AGPS.

[25] Australian Institute of Health and Welfare (1996) *Australia's Health 1996. The fifth biennial health report of the Australian Institute of Health and Welfare*. Canberra: AGPS.

[26] Barresi, C. and Stull, D. (1993) Ethnicity and Long-term Care: An Overview. In *Ethnic Elderly and Long-term Care* (ed. by C. Barresi and D. Stull), pp. 3-21. New York: Springer.

[27] Barro, R.J. (1991) Economic Growth in a Cross-Section of Countries. *Quarterly Journal of Economics*, 106, pp. 444-467.

[28] Becker, G.S. (1981) *A Treatise on the Family.* Harvard University Press.

[29] Becker, G.S. and Barro, R.J. (1988) A Reformulation of the Economic Theory of Fertility. *Quarterly Journal of Economics,* 103, pp. 1-26.

[30] Becker, G.S., Murphy, K. and Tamura, R. (1990) Human Capital, Fertility, and Economic Growth. *Journal of Political Economy,* pp. S12-S37.

[31] Beggs, J. and Chapman, B. (1988a) The International Transferability of Human Capital: Immigration Labour Market Outcomes in Australia. In *The Economics of Immigration: The Proceedings of a Conference at the Australian National University, 22-23 April 1987* (ed. by L. Baker and P. Miller), Canberra: AGPS.

[32] Beggs, J. and Chapman, B. (1988b) Immigrant Wage Adjustment in Australia: Cross Section and Time-Series Estimates. *Economic Record,* 64, pp. 161-167.

[33] Berry, A. and Soligo, R. (1969) Some Welfare Aspects of International Migration. *Journal of Political Economy,* 77, pp. 778-794.

[34] Birrell, B. and Khoo, S. (1995) The Second Generation in Australia: Educational and Occupational Characteristics. *BIMPR, Statistical Report* no. 14. Canberra: BIMPR, AGPS.

[35] Borjas, G. (1987) Self-Selection and the Earnings of Immigrants. *The American Economic Review,* 77, pp. 531-553.

[36] Borjas, G. (1991) Immigration Policy, National Origin, and Immigrant Skills: A Comparison of Canada and the United States. *National Bureau of Economic Research Working Paper* no. 3691.

[37] Borjas, G. (1992) The Intergenerational Mobility of Immigrants. *National Bureau of Economic Research Working Paper* no. 3972.

[38] Borjas, G. (1994a) The Economics of Immigration. *Journal of Economic Literature,* XXXII, pp. 1667-1717.

[39] Borjas, G. (1994b) The Economic Benefits from Immigration. *National Bureau of Economic Research Working Paper* no. 4955.

[40] Borjas, G. (1994c) Immigration and Welfare, 1970-1990. *National Bureau of Economic Research Working Paper* no. 4872.

[41] Borjas, G. (1995) The Economic Benefits from Immigration. *Journal of Economic Perspectives,* 9, pp. 3-22.

[42] Borjas, G. and Freeman, R. (eds) (1992) *Immigration and the Workforce: Economic Consequences for the United States and Source Areas.* Chicago: University of Chicago Press.

[43] Borjas, G. and Hilton, L. (1995) Immigration and the Welfare State: Immigrant Participation in Means-Tested Entitlement Programs. *National Bureau of Economic Research Working Paper* no. 5372.

[44] Borjas, G. and Trejo, S. (1993) National Origin and Immigrant Welfare Recipiency. *Journal of Public Economics*, 50, pp. 325-344.Borjas, G., Freeman, R. and Katz, L. (1991) On the Labour Market Effects of Immigration and Trade. *National Bureau of Economic Research Working Paper* no. 3761.

[45] Borjas, G., Freeman, R. and Katz, L. (1996) Searching for the Effects of Immigration on the Labour Market. *National Bureau of Economic Research Working Paper* no. 5454.

[46] Borland, J. (1995) Male Labour Market Participation in Australia. *University of Melbourne Department of Economics Research Paper* no. 461.

[47] Borsch-Supan, A., Gokhale, J., Kotlikoff, L. and Morris, J. (1992) The Provision of Time to the Elderly by their Children. In *Topics in the Economics of Aging* (ed. by D. A. Wise), pp. 109-131. Chicago: The University of Chicago Press.

[48] Boyer, E.F. (1987) Ethnicity and Ageing. *Journal of Cross-Cultural Gerontology*, 2, pp.107-113.

[49] Bratsberg, B. (1995) Legal versus Illegal U.S. Immigration and Source Country Characteristics. *Southern Economic Journal*, 61, pp. 715-727.

[50] Bradbury, G., Garde, P. and Vipond, J. (1986) Youth Unemployment and Intergenerational Immobility. *Journal of Industrial Relations*, 28, pp. 191-210.

[51] Brooks, C. and Volker, P. (1985) Labour Market Success and Failure: An Analysis of the Factors Leading to the Workplace Destinations of the Australian Population. In *The Structure and Duration of Unemployment in Australia* (ed. by P. Volker), BLMR Monograph no. 6. Canberra: AGPS

[52] Brooks, C. and Williams, L. (1995) *Immigrants and the Labour Market, the 1990-94 Recession and Recovery in Perspective.* Canberra: BIMPR, AGPS.

[53] Bureau of Immigration, Multicultural and Population Research (1995) *Australian Immigration, Consolidated Statistics.* Canberra: BIMPR, AGPS.

[54] Campos, J. and Lien, D. (1995) Political Instability and Illegal Immigration. *Journal of Population Economics*, 8, pp. 23-33.

[55] Centre for International Economics (1988) *The Relationship Between Immigration and Economic Performance.* In *Immigration: A Commitment to Australia* (CAAIP). Canberra: AGPS.

[56] Centre for International Economics (1992) *Immigration and the Commonwealth Government Budget.* Canberra: AGPS.

[57] Chapman, B. and Salvage, A. (1994) Immigrant Male Wages in Australia: the Role of Education. *Australian National University Centre for Economic Policy Research Discussion Paper* no. 304.

[58] Chesnais, J-C. (1992) *The Demographic Transition, Stages, Patterns, and Economic Implications.* New York: Oxford University Press.

[59] Chiswick, B. (ed.) (1992) *Immigration, Language, and Ethnicity: Canada and the United States.* Washington DC: AEI Press.

[60] Chiswick, B. and Miller, P. (1985) Immigrant Generation and Income in Australia. *Economic Record,* 61, pp. 540-553.

[61] Clarke, H. (1995a) International Labour-Cum-Capital Migrations: Theory, Welfare Implications and Evidence. *La Trobe University Schools of Economics and Commerce Discussion Paper* no. A.95.04.

[62] Clarke, H. (1995b) Australian and Canadian Labour-Cum-Capital Migrations: Push Factors, Causality and the Role of US Labour Intakes. *La Trobe University Schools of Economics and Commerce Discussion Paper* no. A.95.07.

[63] Clarke, H. (1995c) UK Labour Emigrations and Capital Exports 1816-1991. *La Trobe University Schools of Economics and Commerce Discussion Paper* no. A.95.08.

[64] Clarke, H. (1995d) International Populations: Some Welfare Implications of Birth, Death and Migration. *La Trobe University Schools of Economics and Commerce Discussion Paper* no. A.95.05.

[65] Clarke, H. and Martin, V. (1995) Does Capital Chase Labour Internationally? *La Trobe University Schools of Economics and Commerce Discussion Paper* no. A.95.11.

[66] Clarke, H. and Ng, Y-K. (1991) Are There Valid Economic Grounds for Restricting Immigration? *Economic Papers,* 10, pp. 71-76.

[67] Clarke, H. and Ng, Y-K. (1993) Immigration and Economic Welfare: Resource and Environmental Aspects. *Economic Record,* 69, pp. 259-273.

[68] Clarke, H. and Ng, Y-K. (1995) Population Growth and the Benefits from Optimally Priced Externalities. *Australian Economic Papers,* 34.

[69] Clarke, H. and Smith, L. (1995) Labour Immigration and Capital Flows: Long-Term Australian, Canadian and United States Experience. *La Trobe University Schools of Economics and Commerce Discussion Paper* no. A.95.10.

[70] Clarke, H., Chisholm, A.H., Edwards, G.W., and Kennedy, J.O.S. (1990) *Immigration, Population Growth and the Environment*. Canberra: AGPS.

[71] Commonwealth Department of Community Services and Health, Policy Development Division (1990) *The Impact of Population Ageing on Commonwealth and State Social Outlays 1987-1988*. Canberra: AGPS.

[72] Commonwealth of Australia (1996) *Budget Statements 1996-97, Budget Paper No. 1*. Canberra: AGPS.

[73] Cowgill, D. (1974) Ageing and Modernization: A Revision of the Theory. In *Later Life: Communities and Environmental Policy* (ed. by J. Gubrium). Springfield, Ill: Charles C. Thomas.

[74] Cowgill, D. (1986) *Ageing Around the World*. Belmont, Ca: Wadsworth.

[75] Creedy, J. and Disney, R. (1985) *Social Insurance in Transition: An Economic Analysis*. Oxford: Clarendon Press.

[76] Creedy, J. and Disney, R. (1992) Financing State Pensions in Alternative Pay-as-you-go Schemes. *Bulletin of Economic Research*, 44, pp. 39-53.

[77] Creedy, J. and Taylor, P. (1993a) Population Ageing and Social Expenditure in Australia. *Australian Economic Review*, 3'93, pp. 44-56.

[78] Creedy, J. and Taylor, P. (1993b) The Coming of Age in Australia: Some Further Results. *University of Melbourne Department of Economics Research Paper* no. 373.

[79] Cropper, M. and Griffiths, C. (1994) The Interaction of Population Growth and Environmental Quality. *American Economic Review*, 84, pp. 250-254.

[80] Cutler, D., Poterba, J., Sheiner, L. and Summers, L. (1995) An Aging Society: Opportunity or Challenge. In *The Economics of Ageing* (ed. by J. Creedy), pp. 169-227. Aldershot: Edward Elgar.

[81] Cutts, L. (1992) *Immigration and Local Government Budgets*. Canberra: AGPS.

[82] Daniger, S., van der Gaag, J., Smolensky, E. and Taussig, M. (1982) The Life Cycle Hypothesis and the Consumption Behaviour of the Elderly. *Journal of Post Keynesian Economics*, 5, pp. 208-227.

[83] Dasgupta, P. (1993) *An Inquiry into Well-being and Destitution.* Oxford: Clarendon.

[84] Dasgupta, P. (1995) The Population Problem: Theory and Evidence. *Journal of Economic Literature*, XXXIII, pp. 1879-1902.

[85] De New, J. and Zimmermann, K. (1993) Blue Collar Labour Vulnerability: Wage Impacts of Migration. *Universitat Munchen Volkswirtschaftlichen Fakultat Research Paper* no. 93-22.

[86] Department of Employment, Education and Training (1995) *Australia's Workforce 2005: Jobs in the Future.* Canberra: AGPS.

[87] Department of Immigration and Ethnic Affairs (1994) *Settler Arrivals and Permanent Departures by Birthplace, Age and Gender 1988/89-1992/93.* Special data request.

[88] Department of Social Security (1995a) DSS Payment Statistics. Unpublished.

[89] Department of Social Security (1995b) Annual Report 1994-95. Canberra: AGPS.

[90] Economic Planning Advisory Council (1988) Economic Effects of an Ageing Population. Council Paper no. 29.

[91] Economic Planning Advisory Council (1994) Australia's Ageing Society. Background Paper no.37. Canberra: AGPS.

[92] Economic Planning Advisory Council (1996) Future Labour Market Issues for Australia. Commission Paper no. 12. Canberra: AGPS.

[93] *Economist* (1996) The Economics of Ageing. *The Economist*, 338.

[94] Evans, M. and Kelley, J. (1986) Immigrants' Work: Equality and Discrimination in the Australian Labour Market. *Australian and New Zealand Journal of Sociology*, 22, pp. 187-207.

[95] Feldstein, M. (1974) Social Security, Induced Retirement, and Aggregate Capital Accumulation. *Journal of Political Economy*, 82, pp. 905-926.

[96] Feldstein, M. (1996) The Missing Piece in Policy Analysis: Social Security Reform. *American Economic Review*, 86, pp. 1-14

[97] Ferguson, B. (1995) Labour Force Substitution and the Effects of an Ageing Population. In *The Economics of Ageing* (ed. by J. Creedy), pp. 273-285. Aldershot: Edward Elgar.

[98] FitzGerald, V.W. (1993) *National Saving: A Report to the Treasurer.* Canberra: AGPS.

[99] Flatau, P. and Hemmings, P. (1991) *Labour Market Experience, Education and Training of Young Immigrants in Australia.* Canberra: BIR,AGPS.

[100] Flatau, P., Petridis, R. and Wood, G. (1995) *Immigrants and Invisible Underemployment.* Canberra: BIMPR, AGPS.

[101] Fogel, R.W. (1994) Economic Growth, Population Theory, and Physiology: The Bearing of Long-Term Processes on the Making of Economic Policy. *American Economic Review*, 84, pp. 369-395.

[102] Foster, W. and Baker, L. (1991) *Immigration and the Australian Economy.* Canberra: BIR, AGPS.

[103] Friedberg, R.M. and Hunt, J. (1995) The Impact of Immigrants on Host Country Wages, Employment and Growth. *Journal of Economic Perspectives*, 9, pp. 23-44.

[104] Fries, J.F. (1980) Ageing, Natural Death and the Compression of Morbidity. *New England Journal of Medicine*, 303, pp. 130-135.

[105] Funkhouser, E. and Trejo, S. (1993) The Decline in Immigrant Labor Market Skills: Did It Continue in the 1980s? *University of California at Santa Barbara Department of Economics Working Paper* no. 1-93.

[106] Galor, O. and Weil, D. (1996) The Gender Gap, Fertility and Growth. *American Economic Review*, 86, pp. 374-387.

[107] Gang, I. and Rivera, F. (1994) Labour Market Effects of Immigration in the United States and Europe: Substitution vs. Complementarity. *Journal of Population Economics*, 7, pp. 157-175.

[108] Green, D. (1995) Immigrant Occupational Attainment: Assimilation and Mobility Over Time. *University of British Columbia Department of Economics Discussion Paper* no. 95-15.

[109] Gutierrez, D. (1995) *Walls and Mirrors: Mexican Americans, Mexican Immigrants, and the Politics of Ethnicity.* University of California Press.

[110] Hagemann, R. and Nicoletti, G. (1989) Ageing Populations: Economic Effects and Implications for Public Finance. *OECD Department of Economics and Statistics Working Paper* no. 61.

[111] Harding, R. (1995) The Debate on Population and the Environment: Australia in the Global Context. *Journal of the Australian Population Association*, 12, pp. 165-195.

[112] Haveman, R. (1996) Public Finance and Demographic Change: Some Macro- and Micro-Implications. *Journal of Public Finance*, 48, pp. 380-385.

[113] Hawthorne, L. (1994) *Labour Market Barriers for Immigrant Engineers in Australia.* Canberra: BIPR, AGPS.

[114] Heller, P.J., Hemming, R. and Kohnert, P.W. (1986) *Ageing and Social Expenditure in the Major Industrial Countries, 1980-2025.* IMF Washington DC Occasional Paper no.47.

[115] Hellwig, O., King, A., Manning, I. and Perkins, J. (1992) *Immigrant Incomes and Expenditures.* Canberra: AGPS.

[116] Hugo, G. (1994) Demographic and Spatial Aspects of Immigration. In *Australian Immigration, A Survey of the Issues* (ed. by Wooden *et al.*), pp. 30-110. Canberra: BIPR, AGPS.

[117] Hurd, M.D. (1992) Wealth Depletion and Life-Cycle Consumption by the Elderly. In *Topics in the Economics of Aging* (ed. by D. A. Wise), pp. 135-160. The University of Chicago Press.

[118] IMF (1996) *World Economic Outlook May 1996.* Washington DC: International Monetary Fund.

[119] Inglis, P. and Stromback, T. (1986) Migrants' Unemployment: The Determinants of Employment Success. *Economic Record*, 62, pp. 310-324.

[120] Johnson, D. (1991) *The Measurement and Extent of Poverty Among Immigrants.* Canberra: AGPS.

[121] Jones, F.L. (1989) The Recent Employment and Unemployment Experiences of Immigrants in Australia. In *The Challenge of Diversity, Policy Options for a Multicultural Australia* (ed. by J. Jupp), pp.141-151. Canberra: OMA, AGPS.

[122] Jones, F.L. (1992) *Sex and Ethnicity in the Australian Labour Market: the Immigrant Experience.* Canberra: ABS, AGPS.

[123] Junankar, P., Kapuscinski, C., Mudd, W. and Pope, D. (1995) Do Migrants Cause Current Account Deficits? *Australian National University Centre for Economic Policy Research Discussion Paper* no. 328.

[124] Jupp, J. and Kabala, M. (eds) (1993) *The Politics of Australian Immigration.* Canberra: BIR, AGPS.

[125] Kee, P. (1992) *Social and Economic Attainment of Immigrants and Later Generation Australians.* Canberra: AGPS.

[126] Kelley, A.C. (1988) Australia: The Coming of Age. *Australian Economic Review*, 2'88, pp. 27-44.

[127] Kenyon, P. and Wooden, M. (1996) Labour Supply. In *The Changing Australian Labour Market* (ed. by K. Norris and M. Wooden), EPAC Commission Paper No.11, pp. 15-38. Canberra: AGPS.

[128] Knox, D. (1995) The Age Pension: Means Tested or Universal? *Australian Economic Review*, 3'95, pp. 107-110.

[129] Knox, D. (1996) Contemporary Issues in the Ongoing Reform of the Australian Retirement Income System. *Australian Economic Review*, 2'96, pp. 199-210.

[130] LaLonde, R. and Topel, R. (1994) Economic Impact of International Migration and the Economic Performance of Migrants. *University of Chicago Center for the Study of the Economy and the State Working Paper* no. 96.

[131] Lazear, E. (1995) Culture and Language. *National Bureau of Economic Research Working Paper* no. 5249.

[132] Leibfritz, W. and Roseveare, D. (1995) Aging Populations and Government Budgets. *The OECD Observer*, pp. 33-37.

[133] Lindbeck, A. (1995) Hazardous Welfare-State Dynamics. *American Economic Review*, 85, pp. 9-15.

[134] Massey, D. (1995) The New Immigration and Ethnicity in the United States. *Population and Development Review*, 21, pp. 631-652.

[135] Masson, P. and Tryon, R. (1995) Macroeconomic Effects of Projected Population Aging in Industrial Countries. In *The Economics of Ageing* (ed. by J. Creedy), pp. 568-600. Aldershot: Edward Elgar, .

[136] Mathews, R. (1992) *Immigration and State Budgets*. Canberra: AGPS.

[137] McDowell, J. and Singell, L. (1993) An Assessment of the Human Capital Content of International Migrants: An Application to U.S. Immigration. *Regional Studies*, 27, pp. 351-363.

[138] Meikle, K. and Tulpule, A. (1985) Government Expenditure. In *The Economic Effects of Immigration in Australia* (ed. by N. Norman and K. Meikle), Melbourne: CEDA.

[139] Miller, P. (1986) Immigrant Unemployment in the First Year of Australian Labour Market Activity. *Economic Record*, 62, pp. 82-87.

[140] Miller, P. and Volker, P. (1987) The Youth Labour Market in Australia: A Survey of Issues and Evidence. *Australian National University Centre for Economic Policy Research Discussion Paper no. 171*.

[141] Minas, I., Lambert, T., Kostov, S. and Boranga, G. (1996) *Mental Health Services for NESB Immigrants, Transforming Policy into Practice*. Canberra: AGPS.

[142] Moore, W., Newman, R. and Fheili, M. (1992) Measuring the Relationship between Income and NHEs. *Health Care Financing Review*, 14, pp. 133-139.

[143] National Population Council (1991) *Population Issues and Australia's Future*. Canberra: AGPS.

[144] Neal, L. (1978) Is Secular Stagnation Just around the Corner? A Survey of the Influences of Slowing Population Growth upon Investment Demand. In *The Economic Consequences of Slowing Population Growth* (ed. by T. Espenshade and W Serow), pp. 101-126. New York Academic Press.

[145] Norris, K. and Wooden, M. (1995) The Changing Australian Labour Market: An Overview. In *The Changing Australian Labour Market* (ed. by K. Norris and M. Wooden), pp. 1-14. Commission Paper no. 11. Canberra: EPAC, AGPS.

[146] Notestein, F.W. (1953) Economic Problems of Population Change. *Proceedings of the Eighth International Conference of Agricultural Economists*, pp. 13-31. New York: Oxford University Press.

[147] OECD (1994) *The OECD Jobs Study, Evidence and Explanations, Part I - Labour Market Trends and Underlying Forces of Change*. Paris: OECD.

[148] OECD (1995a) *OECD Economic Outlook*. Paris: OECD.

[149] OECD (1995b) *OECD Economic Surveys, Australia*. Paris: OECD.

[150] Office of the Australian Government Actuary (1991) *Australian Life Tables 1985-1987*. Canberra: AGPS.

[151] Parr, N. and Mok, M. (1995) Differences in the Educational Achievements, Aspirations and Values of Birthplace Groups in New South Wales. *People and Place,* 3, pp. 1-8.

[152] Pearce, A., Bertone, S. and Stephens, J. (1995) *Surviving Retrenchment, Experiences of NESB Immigrant Workers in the Western Region of Melbourne*. Canberra: BIMPR, AGPS.

[153] Peter, M. and Verikios, G. (1994) Quantifying the Effect of Immigration on Economic Welfare in Australia. *Monash University Department of Economics Seminar Paper* no. 13/94.

[154] Pischke, J. and Velling, J. (1994) Wage and Employment Effects of Immigration to Germany: An Analysis Based on Local Labour Markets. *Massachusetts Institute of Technology Department of Economics Working Paper* no. 94-8.

[155] Price, C. (1989) *Ethnic Groups in Australia*. Canberra: Immigration Research Centre.

[156] Price, C. (1993) Australia as Intermediary with Asia: A Demographic View. *Journal of Intercultural Studies*, 14, pp. 19-32.

[157] Razin, A. and Sadka, E. (1995) Resisting Migration: Wage Rigidity and Income Distribution. *Centre for Economic Policy Research Discussion Paper* no. 1091.

[158] Rosenman, L. and Warburton, J. (1996) The Changing Context of Retirement in Australia. *Social Security Journal*, pp. 54-56.

[159] Rowland, D.T. (1991a) *Ageing in Australia.* Melbourne: Longman Cheshire.

[160] Rowland, D.T. (1991b) *Pioneers Again: Immigrants and Ageing in Australia.* Canberra: AGPS.

[161] Schmertmann, C. (1992) Immigrants' Ages and the Structure of Stationary Populations with Below-Replacement Fertility. *Demography*, 29, pp. 595-612.

[162] Schultz, T.P. (1988) Economic Demography and Development. In *The State of Development Economics: Progress and Perspectives* (ed. by G. Ranis and T.P. Schultz), pp. 416-451. Oxford: Basil Blackwell.

[163] Schultz, T.P. (1994) Human Capital, Family Planning, and their Effects on Population Growth. *American Economic Review*, 84, pp. 255-260.

[164] Shu, J., Khoo, S.E., Struik, A. and Mckenzie, F. (1994) *Australia's Population Trends and Prospects 1993.* Canberra: BIPR, AGPS.

[165] Shu, J., Goldlust, J., Mckenzie, F., Struik, A. and Khoo, S.E (1996) *Australia's Population Trends and Prospects 1995.* Canberra: BIPR, AGPS.

[166] Simon, J. (1981) *The Ultimate Resource.* New York: Princeton University Press.

[167] Simon, J. (1989) *The Economic Consequences of Immigration.* Oxford: Basil Blackwell.

[168] Stromback, T. (1988) *Migrants, Ethnic Groups and the Labour Market.* Policy Options Paper prepared for the Office of Multicultural Affairs, Canberra.

[169] Stromback, T. and Preston, A. (1991) *The Costs of Low Levels of English Proficiency Amongst Immigrants in the Workforce.* Canberra: AGPS.

[170] Timmer, C.P. (1994) Population, Poverty, and Policies. *American Economic Review*, 84, pp. 261-265.

[171] Tu, P. (1991) Migration: Gains or Losses. *Economic Record*, 67, pp. 153-157.

[172] Usher, D. (1977) Public Property and the Effects of Migration upon Other Residents of the Migrants' Countries of Origin and Destination. *Journal of Political Economy*, 85, pp. 1001-1020.

[173] Wattenberg, B. (1987) *The Birth Dearth.* New York: Pharos Books.

[174] Weber, R. and Straubhaar, T. (1994) Budget Incidence of Immigration into Switzerland: A Cross-Section Analysis of the Public Transfer System. *CEPR Discussion Paper* no. 934.

[175] Weil, D. (1989) *Age and Saving in Micro and Macro Data.* Boston, Mass: Harvard University Press.

[176] Welch, F. (1995) Effects of Cohort Size on Earnings: The Baby Boom Babies' Financial Bust. In *The Economics of Ageing* (ed. by J. Creedy), pp. 228-260. Aldershot: Edward Elgar.

[177] Will, L. (1996) Immigrants Earnings Change: the Importance of Australian Schooling. *ANU Centre for Economic Policy Research Discussion Paper* no. 340.

[178] Winocur, S., Rosenman, L. and Warburton, J. (1994) *The Retirement Decisions of Non-English Speaking Background Women.* Canberra: BIPR, AGPS.

[179] Wooden, M. (1990) *Migrant Labour Market Status.* Canberra: AGPS.

[180] Wooden, M. and Robertson, F. (1989) *The Factors Associated with Migrant Labour Market Status.* Canberra: BIR, AGPS

[181] Wooden, M., Holton, R., Hugo, G. and Sloan, J. (1994) *Australian Immigration: A Survey of the Issues.* Canberra: BIPR, AGPS.

[182] World Bank (1994) *Averting the Old Age Crisis.* New York: Oxford University Press.

[183] Young, C. (1988) Towards a Population Policy: Myths and Misconceptions Concerning the Demographic Effects of Immigration. *Australian Quarterly*, 60, pp. 220-230.

[184] Young, C. (1990) *Australia's Ageing Population: Policy Options.* Canberra: AGPS.

[185] Young, C. (1994) Beliefs and Realities about the Demographic Role of Immigration. *Australian Quarterly*, 66, pp. 49-74.

Index